Dan Shanahan

Waiting for Something That Never Arrived

*Meditations on a Progressive America
in Honor of Tony Judt*

polemos

320.11
11/11

Dan Shanahan
Waiting for Something That Never Arrived.
Meditations on a Progressive America in Honor of Tony Judt

Published by TOGGA®, publishing house,
Volutová 2524/12, 158 00 Prague, Czech Republic
in series **polemos**

www.togga.cz

This book is published under the auspices of the research project 35/DPV/2011
undertaken at the Charles University in Prague, Faculty of Humanities

Copyright © Dan Shanahan, 2011
Editor: Thomas O'Hearn
Cover design: Lukáš Příbaň
Layout & typesetting: Dušan Neumahr
Typeface: Comenia by Tomáš Brousil, Radana Lencová and František Storm
Printed by: Tiskárna PROTISK, s. r. o.,
České Budějovice, Czech Republic
All rights reserved
The first edition, Prague 2011
ISBN 978-80-87258-61-3
Library of Congress Control Number: 2011934918

For Gabriel, Daniel, Marc and Nicholas

For much of mankind the dread of famine had all but disappeared in a majestic world food market; modern medicine had made pestilence unlikely, had improved the health of millions, had postponed Death himself, and might, so some men speculated, bring the death of Death. But new and nagging worries, a sense of waiting for something that never arrived, seemed to have replaced those dreads, now that man looked not to eternity and bliss for himself but for a future time of prosperity either for himself or his descendants.

Stringfellow Barr
The Pilgrimage of Western Man

Introductory

As was the case for so many other readers of *The New York Review of Books*, the January 14, 2010 issue hit me like a thunderclap. In that issue, Tony Judt's "Night" revealed what those close to him had known for some time: he had been diagnosed with amyotrophic lateral sclerosis—Lou Gherig's Disease, as it is more commonly known in the US—and was already suffering the condition's advanced symptoms, virtual quadraplegia. Moreover, the disease was fatal; the life expectancy from the time of diagnosis—October of 2008 in Tony's case—was two years.[1]

I had had brief email contact with Tony Judt in 2003 about an article in the *NYRB* in which he had characterized remarks Vaclav Havel had made about the United States. At the time, I thought he had slightly misunderstood the remarks and offered my interpretation of them; Tony's response convinced me he had, indeed, understood what Havel was trying to say. But more striking about the 3–4 message exchange was the genuine, even warm collegiality with which he responded, both to my remarks and to an article of mine about the 9/11 attacks I attached

---

1   "Night" appeared in the UK in the January 9 edition of *The Guardian*.

to one of the messages. In the brief period of that contact, I felt I had encountered a mind genuinely engaged by issues that meant a great deal to him, but also willing to discuss those issues with anyone who shared his engagement with them. Put simply, Tony's messages "had heart".

So "Night" came as a double blow: the diagnosis portended, not only the stilling of one of the most vibrant and insightful progressive voices on either side of the Atlantic—and one who had shown no small amount of courage in the face of some of the harsh attacks his honesty had sometimes provoked—it also represented a death sentence for someone who had, however briefly, taken on real flesh-and-blood presence in my life.

Initially, I felt the urge to write him a message of support, but I held off, knowing that the advanced stage of his disease meant normal communication would consume an inordinate amount of his time. Then, quite by accident, I discovered that a close friend and colleague of many years had attended Emanuel School with Tony and that the two of them were exchanging reminiscences of their school days. Emboldened by the coincidence, I wrote a message which included the following remarks about *Ill Fares the Land*, which I had just finished:

> As a 21-year American expatriate—13 years in Paris, 8 years here in Prague—and a military kid until I was sixteen, I am probably as much an "edge person" as anyone, so it was particularly interesting to read your analysis of the country I left behind, most especially since we each stand in much the same relation to the countries where we live. However, as I read, I found myself in the

perplexing position of wondering if you weren't leaving yourself open to the accusation of naiveté with respect to your assessment of the possibilities of social democracy in America.

Understand, this is a genuine, not a rhetorical "wonder". Though yearly trips back "home"—and now the ubiquity of the internet—have kept me in touch with what's gone on in the US in the time since I left, I'm acutely aware of the fact that I'm cut off from the hundred and one nuances that give one the real flavor of what's going on. That can be a blessing at times (I dodged the real acerbity of the OJ trial, the Lewinski scandal and the Bush years); but it forces you to admit that your perceptions are all second-hand.

Moreover, I've never been a knee-jerk pessimist. My time in Sacramento in the heady, late 60s was punctuated by stays at SF State, living in the Haight-Ashbury; and in the long trough that followed I remained hopeful that the Baby Boomers would once again find their voice and become a force for progressive change. (The rejection of Reagan's attempts to ally the US with the Contras was the last time I remember thinking that their voice had returned.) But once I made the move to Europe, I ceased to anticipate that return—something I realized only while reading *Ill Fares*. Thus, what had at first struck me as an intriguing cross-cultural exercise (reading a book about America by an expatriate Brit) became an unexpected exploration of the many subliminal, or simply unarticulated, assumptions about America I had made in my two decades abroad. And I was surprised to find the degree to which they were pessimistic.

I won't go into great detail about the sources of that pessimism. Most recently I've been reading Richard Hofsteder, J.W. Cash and Faulkner out of a hunch that the "red-blue" split in

America has its origins in some amalgam of anti-intellectualism and Southern exceptionalism—the sub-text being that America can't enter the social democratic universe Europe has because it's still fighting the Civil War. And I'm always ready to be proven wrong, especially when the consequences may be that I can encourage my sons, rather than hold my breath, when they speculate about living their adult lives in America. (Not that living in the world of [Vaclav] Klaus and rampant post-communist opportunism is much better; but it is, a bit.)

But at bottom I don't see anything like the critical mass there that, for instance, made the New Deal attitudes possible. While I found myself agreeing with practically every point you made, at the same time I found myself unable to imagine more than a handful of readers being ready to take up what is essentially a call to action. (Sadly, I can't imagine more than a handful of Americans taking up the book itself, though I've recommended it to one old Stanford acquaintance who recently dismissed "European-style socialism" as "too much government".)

Of course, offering hope is something we all want to do when we offer a critique—and something that has always, to my mind, been a serious shortcoming on the Left in America; and were I to write a book like this I'd probably build it on some kind of "yes we can" foundation, however tempered. So perhaps what my wondering really boils down to is whether your implied optimism is a necessary rhetorical stance, or whether there may be things (attitudes, audiences, "players") you see that I cannot, either by virtue of the fact that you sit on one edge, I on another—or some combination of the two?

Tony's response, both gracious and warm, began another brief—this time tragically brief—exchange between us. Writing in abbreviated fashion because of his disease, he confessed that *Ill Fares the Land* had been far better received in countries like Germany and the Netherlands than in the US; I responded with some thoughts about the role of the American Dream in past progressive achievements, as well as some reflections on George Lakoff's work, and he asked me to keep writing my thoughts whenever I had the time: these were matters that continued to engage him; he wanted to see where I was going with them.

Over the course of three months I wrote Tony two further sets of reflections, but had many more in mind. The experience was both exhilirating and chilling. I had not had the chance to discuss the underlying currents in American society, particularly in its politics, for many years, let alone with a mind of the breadth and depth of Tony's. Nor had I ever had the opportunity to share reflections with someone who, like me, lived life with the special perspective that having been an "outsider"—an "edge person", as he put it—gives. Working around my cottage, biking through the Southern Bohemian hills, the opportunity to share my thoughts, and to benefit from the few his disease would allow him to pass on, gave the prospect of this conversation a special aura.

But it was an aura colored by the death sentence under which Tony lived. I knew the conversation could come to an abrupt halt at any time, and I clung to the hope that, as I put it in my first message to him, "the British intellect contains some enzyme that has allowed Stephen Hawking to hang on, and that you will too".

Sadly, and all too predictably, that was not the case. In early August, I sent a long message about Herbert Croly's *The Promise of American Life*, and ten days later was about to send another longer set of reflections about Lakoff, when I opened the *New York Times'* obituary webpage to see the announcement of Tony's death.

Beyond the thoughts about his family, his colleagues, the many books and articles I had expected to read for years to come that would never be, there was a strange, vaccuous feeling that engulfed me through the rest of the summer. As I worked and rode through the rest of August into September, I found myself caught up in the same process of reflection that had occupied me in June and July, but now without the prospect I'd once had of sharing the products of that process. It felt a bit like having been cut off in the middle of a telephone conversation, or losing a half-finished article to a computer crash. But lost text can be reconstructed, interrupted telephone calls continued another time. There was no way to reconstruct a partner—even one whose disease had consigned him to a largely passive role— once he or she has disappeared. But try as I might, I couldn't bring my end of the conversation to a close. And, as the summer drew to an end, and the thoughts continued to percolate out, I realized that there was only one thing to do: I would write one, long message that would sum up all the thoughts I could no longer share with Tony. They would, rather Proust-like, I suspect he might say, become this book.

I cannot say how Tony might have responded, had the conversation continued, to what I've said here. My intuition is that he would have agreed with much, if not most of what is said. Perhaps the best indication of how he would have resonded lies in a remark he had made, over ten years ago in, *Beyond Responsibility: Blum, Camus, Aron and the French Twentieth Century*. Speaking of the French intellectuals who dominated the political discourse of those times, he said they had a tendency to reflect and echo in the most conventional way the political and cultural fissures and conflicts around them, rather than contributing to the redirection of national attention on to other, more promising tracks.

These words might easily have been written with the progressive political discourse of the last three decades in mind. For, whatever the prospects might be for a coalescence of progressive attitudes into a viable political force in Western democracies—and it must be said that the "Yes we can" moment of the 2008 American presidential election was an indication, however brief, that such a coalescence can still take place—no substantive change can take place without the introduction of a "redirection of attention" among progressives in Western democracies. The old, hackneyed phrases which the left relies on inspire no one, and as George Lakoff has suggested, what little persuasive power they may have pales before the manipulative phrase-making the right has used so successfully since the Reagan-Thatcher era.[2]

---

2   Those unfamiliar with George Lakoff's work might begin with his *Moral Politics: How Liberals and Conservatives Think* (Chicago: University of Chicago Press, 2002).

But the redirection of attention will not accomplish anything if it does not go deeper than a mere recrafting of "message". The simple truth is that progressives have, to an alarming extent, lost their way. The term progressive itself has fallen into disuse, because no one knows anymore what "progress" is: many suspect it was a convenient fiction to hide rampant exploitation of resources, human and otherwise; others feel it is simply too problematic a term to allow into the political discussion—who's progress, and for what?

Thus a much deeper "redirection" is called for. Progressives must ask themselves, not whether justice and equity remain the basis for their beliefs—that is taken for granted—but how that belief situates itself in the pass to which humanity has come in the late 20th and early 21st century. What does it mean to have the resources to eliminate vast amounts of human suffering but to lack the infrastructure to do so? We have come, as one commercial used to say, a long way: but *what does where we've come from tell us about where we must next go?* This book is, quite simply, an attempt to redirect our attention to some of these questions and towards the notion of building a unified world view that will help us to begin answering them systematically.

Some would say these are philosophical—or anthropological—questions at best and cannot be addressed in the context of contemporary politics. But I disagree. And the all too brief discussion Tony and I engaged in before his death tells me that, whether or not he would have agreed with the outline I've set down here, he would most certainly have been engaged by the prospect of wrestling with these questions, debating them, and exploring the paths they opened up. I have no doubt that he would have been able to refine and sharpen many of the ideas I have painted in broadstroke, and my intuition is that he would have shared many of them. Thus, while the ideas are mine and mine alone, he must get credit for encouraging them in the way only a good and engaged listener can.

For having been that listener and having been so engaged with the concerns he and I—and many others—shared, he has earned my deepest gratitude.

I

We have to begin with premises.

Long ago, before the world was awash with deconstruction, the American philosopher Susanne Langer said that how one formulates one's enquiries reveals one's attitude of mind. That's a remark that can be used to unmask, unveil or underpin. In the first case, you have today's vast industry of deconstruction, stripping away the naïve, negligent and self-serving layers of assumptions that so often give our world its shape: the assumption that men outrank women underlying our everyday language; the condescension inherent in much of what we say about other countries and other cultures; the way history has been fashioned and refashioned to veil some of its darker truths. In the second, perhaps more nuanced case, you have the worlds of psychology, literary interpretation or anthropology, to name but a few, in which ferreting out what lies beneath the surface of our conflicts allows us to more deeply understand them and ourselves—and, hopefully, to lead better lives.

But there is a third, least common and little remarked way in which Langer's remark can be used: to construct the world view we want in order to underpin what we do. In some respects, it's like writing a constitution; by establishing our premises, we say, in effect, "We hold these truths to be self evident", and we move on from those truths to the plan of action we build upon them.

The problem is, we hardly ever do this. And nothing could be more true of progressive politics today. Espousing—or opposing—issues and action on the basis of everything from social justice to individual freedom, progressives rarely bother to go beneath the surface of these, our "self-evident truths". And, as a result, we end up with a laundry list of touchstones upon which we try to base our arguments and our plans of action. Moreover, because we shy away from even the notion of "truth", cautious about imposing our truths on others, we often end up with little more than our intuition, or hackneyed notions of injustice, upon which to construct a position: female circumcision is wrong because it is an assault on women, not because the inflicting of suffering by a culture on it own members is as wrong as another culture inflicting suffering on them.

So, perhaps we need to begin by establishing this premise: there *are* truths to which we must all subscribe. They may be few, and there may be circumstances in which their truth value takes on a different shade or texture; but they do exist.

If I take an assault rifle and mow down a dozen passersby on the street, those with mortal wounds will cease to exist, and I will have done them an injustice. Perhaps one of them will have just come from a doctor's office where he or she has been told that, despite the fact that they have an incurable debilitating disease which will cause them and their loved ones years of agony, untold medical expenses, and then end in death, they will have to wait patiently for that end because the law does not permit assisted suicide. Perhaps that one person, who has been searching for a brave and caring medical professional to help them, will be done a justice by my attack. But that rare and unlikely set of circumstances doesn't change the *truth* that attacks on innocent civilians with assault rifles are an injustice, that the lives taken will cease to exist, and that therein lies a violation of some fundamental human value.

But, some will say, if an assault rifle attack on innocent civilians violates some fundamental human value, what about abortion?

Let me say at the outset that I don't like abortion: I don't like the idea of extinguishing life. I make exceptions for mosquitoes and flies, for mice when they begin to overrun my cottage, and I do eat the flesh of dead animals. But in each of those cases it takes very little for me to feel a twinge of pain about the extinguishing of life, no matter how fed up I may be with the bites, the buzzing, or the pointlessly chewed electric cords in the kitchen. All the more so when I think about a potential human life (I emphasize "potential") that is lost when the life of a human embryo is ended: the joys and the sorrows, the dreams and the hopes that will never be. But I support a woman's right to abortion for the simple reason that her body is *her* life, not mine or the state's or the embryo's – just as the body and the life of a suffering and terminally ill patient belongs to the patient. The human life that *is* supercedes the life that may be, and if the mother does not wish to risk her life for that of the embryo, that decision is hers to make, just as the choice to end a life of pointless suffering belongs to the person who is suffering. (For those who feel that the woman who chooses her own life over that of the embryo is selfish, imagine a woman with two young children—a single mother, perhaps—for whom carrying a child to term might prove fatal: is her decision to abort selfish? And could we ever devise legislation that would cover the innumerable "special cases" like this that may arise?)

Many—perhaps most—on the right of the political spectrum will disagree with much of what has been said in that last paragraph. What is remarkable, however, is that most on either the left or the right would not disagree that human life has value. In fact, though saying so may seem a strange way to begin a discussion about building a foundation for progressive politics in the 21st century, there seems to be only one, irreducible statement we can make about the nature of the world as seen through the eyes of our species: life struggles to survive and to perpetuate itself—and, by extension, so do we. Freud argued that there is a complement to the life instinct, *thanatos*; but we have never found more than interpretive evidence that it exists. In contrast, from the flight of a common housefly at the approach of a fly-swatter, to the organization of vast survival plans in such dystopian visions as *Dr. Strangelove* and *2012*, the environment is so rich with instances of the instinct to survive that one is hard pressed to do anything but admit that this is, indeed, a Truth.

So let us begin there. For reasons that we have yet to uncover—and which we may never uncover, at least in the way we have uncovered "reasons" for the appearance of matter in the universe or the emergence of the American Civil Rights movement in the 1950s and 60s—life as we know it struggles to survive and to perpetuate itself; and being one instance of life, so do we. This must be the first premise—the first principle—upon which progressive political thinking builds itself if it is to be true to the world humans inhabit.

But there is a corollary to this principle that must be included in our thinking. For not only does life try to survive and propagate itself, the combination of the two has produced another of those truths which we must admit to be self-evident: life *evolves*. In the simplest terms, life's struggle to survive enters a symbiotic relationship with the dangers inherent in its environment and produces *adaptations* which allow it to do a slightly better job of surviving than it did in the past: single-cell organisms giving way to multi-celled, fins and flippers to feet and wings, and so on. This is, in effect, a second-tier truth that provides us with a fork in the road with respect to establishing our premises. For the fact that life's effort to survive produces evolutionary change means that, taken in its broad sweep, life appears to *progress*. At the very least, life moves from lesser to greater complexity; at another level, it moves to more elaborate coping strategies in its struggle to survive. But that brings us to a fundamental question: is the evolution that takes place really "progress"? is the move from less elaborate to more elaborate coping strategies "good?"

The Romantics harbored the suspicion that it was not. Idyllic, pre-lapsarian existence represented a mode of life in harmony with itself and its surroundings that we have lost because of "progress". But we have no evidence either that earlier times were really harmonious or that the advance of civilization, as it is often referred to, is a move away from some kind of equilibrium. While aspects of the Romantics' view lives on in fringe groups that would like to eliminate technological advancement—and one must include many religious fundamentalists who, mostly inconsistently, display a similar conviction that we live in a "fallen" state—we can only honestly affirm one thing: whatever disadvantages may have come with life's development of more elaborate coping mechanisms, *that elaboration has brought about the possibility of managing life's interaction with its environment to the benefit of both.*

This is no anthropological or environmental platitude. Faced with the broad sweep of life as we know it, we must admit 1) that it strives to survive, 2) that it adapts itself to its environment,

3) that consciousness has been the most important consequence (thus far) of that adaptation, and 4) that consciousness has made possible the cognizant husbanding of the environment to maximize life's chances of survival. And in the absence of any corollary evidence to give us direction, we must choose for ourselves between two paths: either the evolution of life's coping strategies, which has produced human consciousness, is an aberrant force (often the fundamentalist's view, and too often sampled by the contemporary right) or it is not.

Though it may seem an act of faith—an intellectual *faux pas* of monumental proportions in today's intellectual climate—the only path a progressive world view can take is to assume that the evolution of life and its coping strategies is, at least, not aberrant or destructive. This may appear to some a Panglossian attitude (what is, must, by virtue of being, be good). But notice we haven't said that the evolution of life is, in and of itself, a good: only that it is not aberrant. This may seem a logical trick, but it's not. We need to be very stingy with the notion of "good", and though some will want to assign it to evolution, that is perhaps a metaphysical step too far. Suffice it to say that if we want to place a value on life's struggle to survive and perpetuate itself, and evolution supports that value, then evolution can be included under the broader umbrella of value life carries with it. Moreover, for anyone who fears the danger of letting a subjective perception (the apparent practical value of evolution for survival) take on too much weight, there is the reassurance provided by the notion that evolution has produced the means—consciousness, reason, good judgment, etc.—to develop strategies for good stewardship of the environment life inhabits; that environment is itself both the absolute objective reality and the precondition for the existence of life as we know it. (And, for the existentialists who may want to factor in the possibility that all our efforts could ultimately be in vain, there is the fact that 1) we may not succeed in developing strategies for good stewardship and 2) a destructive event of cosmic dimensions could reduce our efforts to less than a cosmic footnote.)

To put all of this in a simple metaphor: reality as we know it has an engine; the engine is running, and we are waking up to the fact that we are—at least to some extent—in the driver's seat. Where the road is leading us, we don't quite know. Those who wish to believe that the road is part of some grand, cosmic swirl towards a greater good will find themselves in good company: Einstein counted himself among them. For those (on most days I include myself in this group) who suspect that there may be some grand, benign force unfolding, but who prefer to concentrate on the bumps and curves on the road at hand, less metaphysics and more realism will seem appropriate. For those who believe there is only chaos, and that one must fight the good fight all the same, there is the road and the engine, nothing more. But regardless of which of these positions (or the many others that lie proximate to them) we occupy, we are, by virtue of occupying them, progressives. That is to say, we know there is an engine running, we know that there is movement, we are coming to realize the extent to which we are in the driver's seat—and that *developing our driving skills in a way that will support life and its struggle to survive and propagate itself is what we are about.*

Moreover, for those who may—as I do—harbor some lingering, or even very strong reluctance to jump on board any bandwagon with something analogous to "Progress is our most important product" painted on its side, there are, as we will see, ample circumstances in which 1) we must restrict our notion of what constitutes progress (increase in GDP, for instance, should not qualify in and of itself as a criteria for social progress) and

2) we must value conserving things, from forests to ethnic traditions, that may be threatened by the inevitable surge of evolution in a direction we may tend think of as "forward" because, as George Lakoff would say, we think in terms of paths. Progress is best thought of, paradoxically enough, as a state, but one in which change is the constant. A progressive mind set must distinguish between what change is valuable and what is not. And it must offer forums for discussing and tools for identifying value.

On Happiness

In 1909, Herbert Croly, founder of *The New Republic*, published a progressive manifesto entitled *The Promise of American Life* that had a large impact on progressive thinkers from Theodore Roosevelt right up through the New Deal. In one respect, Croly's view of what must emerge in the 20th century if the progressive vision were to be realized is consonant with what we have said here so far: not surprisingly, it is an extension of the Founders' notion of the "inalienable rights" to "the pursuit of life, liberty and the pursuit of happiness". What is remarkable, however, is the degree to which Croly's vision is both parochial and relatively short-sighted.

The first of these appears in bold-face in the title itself: the promise of which Croly speaks is inherent in *American* life. Understandably, there was perhaps some reluctance to ascribe the dazzling promise of America, circa 1909, to the world at large; but that reluctance itself was no doubt based on a belief that America had a lock on progress—progress understood here as evolution towards an increased standard of living, increased stability and the maintenance of the freedoms to which most Americans were becoming accustomed. There is more than a little self-congratulation in Croly's view of such things as American individualism and, for lack of a better word, stick-to-itiveness. For Croly, the full force of American virtues such as these had been diminished by the injustices, economic and political, of what Mark Twain had labeled "the Gilded Age" of American industrialization. America needed to reform itself, in Croly's view, to continue to shine as the prime example of human progress it had always been.

But of course, Croly does not ask the long-term question—nor perhaps could have anyone of his time—"What then?" Once we have realized the goal of stable material well-being, what next? This question is not asked by Croly, nor by much of anyone else in the first half of the 20th century, and for good reason: the stability of American material well-being was not considered reliable at least until the end of the Second World War—which itself helped to fend off the wolves of economic depression that snarled at the door during the 1930s. But all the same, a vision of what transpires after the millenarian achievement of stable economic well-being was ignored except in the vaguest terms by progressive thinkers of Croly's time and after.

These two shortfalls in Croly's vision are significant because, in the globalized world of the late 20th and now the 21st century, they are not only relevant but related. America can no longer be seen as the prime example of human progress. The biggest, yes; but some would introduce a whole variety of epithets (garish, bullying, immature, ruthless, egotistical, narcissistic, etc.) before even considering its positive accomplishments—which are not few. But even more importantly, in many features of life Croly and his contemporaries would have certainly included in America's "promise", America can no longer even be considered the first among equals: in a whole myriad of ways, from child mortality to education, medical care to distribution of wealth,

America lags behind many industrial democracies. The promise of American life, which was no doubt laced with notions of Manifest Destiny left over from the 19th century, has decidedly *not* kept pace with the promise of material well-being enjoyed by much of the rest of the industrial world. Moreover, the one area in which America clearly does excel, conspicuous consumption, has led to a suspicion that the promise of American life, whatever it was, has either remained unrealized, or worse, that it was a false promise to begin with.

There is a knotted web of changes here that not only radically distinguishes our time from Croly's, but which also points the way towards a shift progressive thinking must make if it is to be truly progressive. The first involves scope.

Croly and his contemporaries were not locked in some myopic illusion of America as the sole force for human progress on the planet. But they clearly saw American life as a discrete entity in a patchwork quilt that ranged from, say, African "primitivism" to American "modernity". There were interactions and even interdependencies, to be sure—rubber, for instance, an increasingly important commodity for the blooming industrial giant, was obtainable largely from these so-called primitive societies. But if the notion of global integration even emerged among policy makers of the time, it was more likely to involve questions surrounding something like the acquisition of the Philippines. Today, we have integrated virtually every feature of life on the planet to a greater or lesser degree—markets and media being the chief forces in that process. We truly inhabit a planet whose integrated features have vastly outdistanced its discrete parts in their importance for our daily lives and our future. Thus, no contemporary progressive vision can claim to be comprehensive unless it establishes itself on foundations applicable to everyone on the globe.

That fact alone will give anyone who is circumspect about traditional notions of progress pause. If we have learned anything in the nearly two-thirds of a century since the end of the Second World War, it is that the imposition of Western values on non-Western societies is to be avoided, both for the benefit of the non-Western societies and the Western societies themselves. At the same time, it is impossible to deny that, as the net of global integration is drawn ever tighter, the policies and actions of any one group have impact far beyond that group, and a truly progressive vision must acknowledge that fact.

The second important distinction between Croly's time and our own might best be characterized in terms of the American Dream and the discontents which seem to have accompanied its apparent realization.

The American Dream—a term which seems to have originated, not during the halcyon days of the American frontier, but in the face of the capitalist catastrophe known as the Great Depression—is in itself a concept difficult to distill. Used in its most conventional sense, it was meant to capture the aspirations of the millions who came to America with the hope of starting life anew and achieving the economic well-being and stability. But of course, for most the realization of those aspirations was directly tied to freedom from the constraints, some overt, some so deeply woven into the fabric of society as to be almost invisible, which characterized life "in the old country". Without the freedom which American life promised, the dream of economic security could not be assured. So Americans, both newly-arrived and of long-standing, came to consider the two, freedom and economic stability, as indivisible from one another—a perfectly reasonable association to make.

But over time the improbable came to pass: the American Dream was not only realized, but virtually institutionalized, for most of the population—African-Americans being a conspicu-ous exception. Certainly from the time of the 1950s on, modest affluence became the expectation of most Americans, a kind of entitlement they felt, provided they contributed their fare share in the form of hard work, loyalty to the spirit of the Dream, and a vague grab-bag of "American values". But the realization of the Dream brought with it a completely unanticipated prob-lem: what to do with the great energy and determination that had originally been channeled into achieving the Dream. After the 1950s, there was no longer the unifying vision of a society of economic promise to be realized: it *had* been realized; and though some shifted their energies towards achieving such things as social justice, most felt they had earned the right to some respite from struggle, some leisure in which to enjoy the fruits of their labors.

But one of the truths about the American Dream that is all but lost in the criticisms to which it has been subjected in the last half century is that it embodied the same, deeply-felt sense of aspiration that fuels all human striving. Hope of deliverance characterized the decision to come to America to make one's way, and for all the darker nuances we have uncovered about what was once portrayed as a shining example of human en-deavor, it remains true that the energy and determination to start life anew ennobled many who felt them. But once the aspi-ration had been achieved, once the need to strive had plateaued, there was nothing to which those who had made the journey could now attach themselves—*except*, almost involuntarily, the same two things that had served as pillars of fire and of smoke along the way: freedom and economic well-being.

But in an affluent industrial democracy such as America had become by the mid-20th century, freedom and economic well-being were givens for most; striving for them could provide little in the way of higher satisfaction that, say, immigrant parents once felt sacrificing their own lives to provide better lives for their children. Yet without any clear goals towards which to direct their aspirations—indeed, with nothing much in the way of aspirations on the landscape at all—most Americans continued on the well-worn path of "upward mobility", imagining that greater and greater material wealth constituted their natural birthright and that *any attempt to interfere with or redirect their efforts in that direction was a violation of their freedom.* Thus has America, in the last half of the 20th century, become a vehicle for consumer culture: the unbridled acquisition of non-essentials which, once acquired, demonstrate to those who own them the degree of freedom they enjoy.

In some respects, this conundrum is one of the central pivots to the 21st century. Americans tout their freedom as their most distinguishing feature and point—though with less and less assuredness—to their material wealth as a sign of their success. Europeans and others make much less noise about their material achievements, and may have a slightly more circumscribed notion of freedom, but they follow closely in the American wake with respect to the indivisibility of the one from the other. Tellingly, one of the most relied-upon sound bites to emerge from the 9/11 attacks was the notion that the perpetrators hated America "for its freedom". As convoluted as this explanation was if taken at face value, it—no doubt unintentionally—contains an element of deeper truth: the fundamentalists, from Muslim to Marxist and back, who oppose "America" often do so because of the unbridled materialism it represents and their conviction that the spread of such materialism threatens to destroy the fabric of their own cultures, religions and ideologies. While their tactics may be murderously pathological, their fears are not unfounded: the siren-song of consumer culture—often misidentified as "Americanization"—has indeed spread like a virus around the globe. In slums on every continent, owner-ship of a ghetto blaster, a pair of Nikes, or an iPod is seen as a sign of status, even when the owner may live in a hut made of scrap construction materials. And even where consumer goods are the product of stable and successful economic growth rather than a desperate attempt to participate in affluence, their acquisition begins to take on a life of its own, sometimes almost independent of the country, culture, religion or language in which it is practiced.

This conundrum is potentially a matter of great complication for political progressives. If, indeed, the achievement of stable economic well-being, combined with the technological innovations which allowed that achievement, produce a world in which pursuit of consumer goods are the natural result, who is to say that it should be otherwise? Most especially, if those who have not yet achieved economic well-being launch themselves on a program that dangles the promise of consumer goods as one of its rewards, is it right for those of us who have seen the emptiness and anomie that can accompany consumer culture to strike a warning chord?

I suspect that, if questions such as these are ever posed at all, answers to them are largely based on liberal guilt: those deprived of the freedom to achieve stable economic well-being have the right to that freedom, to make the choices that come with it, and to deal with the consequences in whatever fashion they see fit when the time comes. There is some wisdom in that approach: the malaise which seems to have infected America in the age of consumer culture has taken root in a society only two or three centuries old and, by contrast with Asian and African societies which go back millennia, culturally very threadbare.

Cultures with a much more richly woven social fabric might be able to resist the wear of consumerism much more effectively, even give it a vivaciousness we in the West can't imagine.

But the early returns (Japan, Korea, pre-Revolution Iran, Latin American countries wherein consumer culture flourishes) are not heartening. Moreover, the hope that older cultures will better survive the stresses of a consumerizing society is only that, a hope. Any progressive mind committed to the improvement of life for everyone will be concerned about how any society, old or new, can resist those stresses, and progressivism will have to present a response to the fundamentalists who wish to use their fears of those stresses to inflame a radical reaction to them. And finally, as has been said already, a progressive political vision must avoid parochialism. The discontents of consumer culture may be most apparent in American society, slightly less so in other industrial democracies; but they seem to be a constant wherever societies of affluence emerge. To simply set them aside as a concern in situations in which they have not yet emerged is to limit the scope of a progressive world view in one of the ways it most needs to be expanded.

But how?

Sociologists, social psychologists, cultural critics, religious figures and others will each have an analysis of the "freedom to consume" conundrum that seems to loom as a dominant feature of modern life. But a political agenda, while it must learn what each of these has to offer, must provide a basis for action: a synthesis of critiques which also opens the door to responding to the problem in more than piecemeal fashion. And it may be that such a synthesis is not so elusive as we might think. For if we agree that progressive thinking must build on the fact that life struggles to survive, propagate itself and, in the bargain, improve its lot, we need only ask ourselves what lies beyond survival and economic stability. And the answer is quite clear: *quality* of life.

It is to that notion that we next turn.

II

The terms such as "economic well-being" and "stability" which were used in the previous chapter are actually more often expressed in a word with broad rhetorical overtones and a deep, sometimes almost religious significance. That word is "prosperity". In fact, for the West the word prosperity arguably resonates with the beginning of the Beginning, when in Genesis Yahweh creates humankind and tells it to "be fruitful and multiply". For an audience living in a land that alternated between rich valleys and arid deserts, the admonishment to "be fruitful" had clear overtones of material well-being and the struggle to achieve it. And the complement to that admonition was the Chosen People's hope of finding, after the years of wandering in the desert, a "land of milk and honey" wherein true prosperity could be established.

Those notions were not lost on the settlers who came to the New World, whether at Jamestown, Plymouth or the thousands of other locales to which immigrants came from the earliest days of migration to North and South America. The Protestant ethic that fueled the most successful and ultimately most influential of those migrations rooted itself deeply in Biblical notions of having been chosen to fulfill a Divine promise, of the need for hard work as a human complement to the promise, and of the entitlement to prosperity as an outcome. The power of that vision in the United States is apparent today in the extent to which the word "prosperity" is often used in political discourse as the grandest, most elevated reference to what, in more conventional settings, may be simply be indicated by words and phrases such as "the state of the economy", "economic growth" or simply "jobs".

But what is prosperity?

Perhaps the best contemporary answer to that question, and one with, again, deep resonances in the way Americans have wanted to see themselves for two centuries, appears in the images contained in Ronald Reagan's famous "It's Morning in America" ads during the 1984 presidential campaign. The ads, indeed, the entire Reagan presidency, were designed to evoke a kind of spirit of renewal in America after the deeply divisive times of the Sixties and Watergate, and the "malaise" of the Carter years. With those "bad times" behind us, the ads promised, and a vibrant and economically conservative administration in place, Americans could wake up to the lives they had left behind and get on with them. The accompanying images were, in some respects, predictable: neighbors in a bright, sunshiny rural America tending their yards, going to work, and greeting each other with beaming smiles. This, the ads implied, was the "promise of American life;" this was the idyll that could be realized if, first and foremost, such things as freedom from government interference, especially in economic life, were established. These happy people, going about their daily lives unimpeded by big government and free from the anxiety and threat of social problems, were the embodiment of prosperity.

Let's leave aside for a moment the fact that these images, cobbed from some late 19th century myth of small-town America, ignored the realities of mind-numbing suburban sprawl, traffic jams, shopping malls and least-common-denominator television "entertainment"—not to mention inner city poverty, increased drug use throughout the population, corporate crime, environmental degradation and world hunger—to name but a few possible omissions. Focus instead on the images themselves in their own right. For they contain the core of what the prosperity implied by the American Dream has meant.

While many Americans are attracted by the wealth that is apparent in the lives of the rich and famous, their frequent near-obsession with the dark underside of that life, with the fall of the apparently successful, from Gatsby to OJ Simpson, makes clear that they know limitless wealth has its costs. And many, if not most, would agree that they would be quite content with life as it is portrayed in the "It's Morning in America" ads. In fact, the idyll contained in those ads holds an understandable attraction for anyone in search of "the good life", whatever they may conceive it to be. But there is a problem with life as it is portrayed in those ads that undermines them even without the addition of a healthy dose of the realities of twentieth, and now twenty-first, century life they ignore. The problem is that the images are un-American.

For while the American Dream may have always held out the hope of a millennial time when the struggle to achieve it would be won and the fruits of that victory bestowed on the deserving, the simple truth is that Americans have never been content with sitting still long enough to enjoy the benefits of their labors. "We work hard and we play hard" is one of the many mantras that point to the fact that American culture has always had a deep strain of what we came to call the "x" personality type: active, aggressive, achieving, restless to the point of being unable to truly enjoy leisure. While it may be just as apparent in the modern version of Bartleby the Scrivener, the "couch potato", the simple truth is that we live in an environment in which activity, striving and achieving set the tone of our lives. The very air we breathe animates us. So the image of a nineteenth century small-town idyll, while it may invoke nostalgia for a time that, if it ever truly existed, only did so briefly, it nonetheless goes against what has been the animus of American life. As Henry Adams once put it, true satisfaction in our lives comes from the struggle to achieve, not in the achievement itself.

Given that America—and, ultimately, if Max Weber is right about the nature of Western capitalism, the West itself—is so deeply rooted in activity and achievement, it should come as no surprise that its animus makes itself felt in everything from the rise of consumer culture, to the carnivorous nature of corporate business and finance, to the increasing involvement in empire-building international conflicts, from Vietnam to Iraq. Nor should one suppose that a mere critique of the ways in which that animus has made itself felt in the last half century would be likely to produce much. Critique has been the avenue of choice for progressive politics for decades, and while it has achieved occasional successes, it has done nothing to change the deeper assumptions underlying the landscape upon which "conspicuous consumption" is built.

Changing that landscape is not beyond the realm of possibility, but any attempt at reshaping it will have to be made on the basis of the terms and players that already exist on the landscape, the hopes and aspirations that characterize it and the fears and frustrations that threaten to darken it even further. Appeals to social justice, while not to be avoided, have rarely been enough to motivate Americans, and recent history sadly suggests similar trends in much European political thinking. Americans *do* have a fairly strong sense of the importance of fair play, and that can and should be invoked at the appropriate moments—usually when the social climate is sufficiently temperate and unthreatening to allow people to make gestures of benevolent inclusiveness—but stronger suits must be played if progressive thinking is to confront the deeper problems which the West now faces.

Which brings us back to prosperity.

Another Reagan-era political ad invited its audience to ask itself, "Are you better off today than you were four years ago?" At the time, this was largely interpreted as a question that had primarily to do with economic well-being ("Do you have a better income, lower taxes, a better home, more consumer goods?" and so on.). But as any good poll-taker or statistician will tell you, open-ended questions like these produce highly diffuse responses: the phrase "better off", while it may orient the listener towards questions of job, purchasing power, prospects for the future, etc., will also evoke more vague and indeterminate notions of well-being which may range from one's satisfaction at work to safety felt walking the streets to frustration over "welfare queens". As often as not, the answer to whether one is better or not will hinge on a gestalt of all of these things and one's perception of whether or not they are being adequately dealt with by those in power.[3]

So too with the notion of prosperity. Prosperity, when used in the more elevated sense of the well-being of society as a whole, evokes notions of satisfaction which the "It's Morn-

---

3   The 2010 US mid-term elections were a case-study in the primacy economic well-being still enjoys—particularly when it is perceived as being under threat.

ing in America" ads tried to capture with their idyll of small-town American life. To prosper, it implies, means more than to enjoy good economic times; it means, as Webster's collegiate puts it, "to flourish and grow strong". And in this sense, it is simply hard to say that America is prospering. Leaving aside the fact that its economic performance has slipped in the last few decades, there remains a pervasive feeling of unease in the lives of most Americans. Whether it is because of fears about the wisdom of walking the streets of most cities after dark, fears of external forces from al Quaeda to the Chinese holders of massive American debt or fears that "something has gone wrong" with the American Dream, few Americans can honestly say that their lives are fully satisfying—except, perhaps in some specialized, pruned down sense, which usually involves including only personal satisfactions. When taken in the broader sense, to include one's life as a citizen/member of society, there are almost always considerable areas of unease and dissatisfaction, whether one occupies the political left, right, or the vast region of the American middle. If we consider prosperity in this broader sense, few could honestly say that America is prospering, whether in the fashion of the "It's Morning in America" ads, the images of wagon trains moving across the American frontier fed to us through so many media or the more hollow claims of slogans like "America leads the way".

But if it is impossible to argue cogently that America is prospering, it is perhaps even more difficult to have a discussion about what constitutes prosperity. Again, if we speak of ourselves as "consumers"—the term that seems to come up with regard to our public selves far more frequently than "citizens" and, except perhaps at election time, more frequently than "voters"—we may be able to say we enjoy very high levels of satisfaction and, therefore, prosperity. But if we speak of ourselves as "citizens" (and the fact that doing so seems awkward speaks volumes about the way we shape our social identities), we are likely to find ourselves at a conceptual impasse about how even to discuss what constitutes prosperity—in which case imagery from the likes of the "It's Morning in America" ads, for all their negligent naiveté, are probably more evocative than anything we can say about family, spiritual well-being, justice, mother or apple pie. And all too frequently, symbolic images, like the latter two, along with the flag, are liable to morph into concrete concerns and issues to fill in the vacuum created by our inability to have the discussion.

No one has been more immobilized by this inability to express what would constitute real prosperity in a modern democracy than the political left. The right has been more than willing to use images which evoke superficial contentment—or all too real discontent and fear—but the left, burdened as it is with the notion that political vision must be based on reasonable, even rational grounds, has floundered about without firm ground upon which to build its vision, reverting all too often to vague calls to social justice and, in moments of futility, invoking liberal guilt. If progressive political thinking is to break through this conundrum, it must find ground for establishing a discussion that avoids substituting quantity for quality, consumption for satisfaction, affluence for true prosperity.

And such a ground exists.

III

For years, psychologists, social workers and even specialists in business and economic development have used to Abraham Maslow's Hierarchy of Needs to help develop a view of how individuals, larger communities and even societies build on the foundations of life at its most basic, thus affording themselves the opportunity to develop at the level of higher order concerns such as values and moral behavior. Maslow begins, much as was suggested above, with the notion that all of us require a modicum of safety and security—the food, shelter and clothing mantra that often appears in analyses of political thinking—and that until these conditions are guaranteed, the need for them will continue to erupt into, even dominate our lives. Once they have been established, the next level of development, personal or social, requires that the individual feel a sense of belonging or membership in a group appropriate to his or her needs. Further on up the pyramid that these features help to construct, lie the needs to have the respect of one's peers and to feel some degree of self-esteem.[4]

---

4   This is a shorthand version of Maslow: he does not, for instance, say that all the features of life on one level must be in place for an individual to experience features of another; but it helps.

Let's stop for a moment and give these elements of Maslow's model some real world values. Perhaps the place to begin is to acknowledge how often, in the modern world whose benefits we sometimes imagine we "all" enjoy, the first level of safety and security are not established, in fact may be far from being so. In the many regions of Africa that have suffered from famine in recent memory—Darfour, Sudan, Niger—whole populations confront the struggle to survive as their chief daily activity; and many fail. In war-torn regions—Bosnia and Kosovo during the 90s, Iraq during the American invasion and the subsequent insurgencies, Sudan—the same is true. But even where there is neither famine nor war, huge segments of the population in any developing country live in urban slums where, though survival at its most basic may not be in immediate question, the median standard of living may represent only a tenuous hold on survival—one that, for instance, even relatively minor aberrations in climate can eliminate. In fact, when we take into account the many ways in which safety and security can be threatened, not temporarily, such as in a natural disaster in a Western country—floods in the south of France, earthquakes in California and the like—but with the indeterminate duration brought on by, say, conventional and guerrilla armed conflict, drug wars or brutal dictatorships, it is safe to say that the *majority* of the world's population, including many people living in industrial democracies, live in circumstances which permanently or regularly fail to meet the basic requirements of Maslow's model.

That fact alone should, in a globalized world, give us pause. But we'll return to it. Let's look for a moment at the next level of need: the sense of belonging. Here we begin to see the extent to which, though Americans imagine themselves at the pinnacle of humankind's struggle to achieve self-sufficiency, we have not necessarily achieved the level of satisfaction that we might expect. Moreover, we also find that the satisfaction of some of the needs in Maslow's hierarchy takes place in a more checkered than step-wise fashion.

Some years ago, around Christmas time, while I was driving along a freeway through one of the suburbs of Paris, I witnessed something that spoke of the complexities of dealing with questions of basic needs in the modern world. In a field adjacent to the freeway, a Romany family—father, mother, two young children and a dog—stood watching as the last remnants of their trailer went up in smoke. A one-room affair of the kind commonly used by Roma families all over Europe, it had obviously caught fire while they were away—the family car stood unharmed close by—perhaps due to a wiring fault. No doubt everything they had had been destroyed. As I passed, I saw an angry look on the father's face, a worried expression on the mother's, and the two children dancing gleefully at the spectacle, undoubtedly working off the anxiety the event caused them.

I felt devastated by what I saw—but only for a moment. For as I imagined what they would do, I realized that, whatever difficulties they faced from the loss of their trailer, they were no doubt part of an extended family that numbered in the dozens, and they would be taken in and cared for until they could get back on their feet. Simply put, they were part of a community that not only gave them a sense of belonging, but would step in and help them materially in times of need. And that kind of solidarity was automatic: it did not represent a gesture of generosity on the part of those who extended help. It just was.

In fact, in many impoverished populations around the world there is that sense of community, of belonging that helps to explain why the suffering of poverty does not necessarily—or at least immediately—lead to psychological devastation, or, alternatively, to armed rebellion. Of course, solidarity and feelings of community can be two-edged swords. The same very genuine and very deep feelings can generate vendettas, infuse crime rings like the Mafia, and, in their most pathological forms, be used to amplify an "us-them" dichotomy of the kind that fueled National Socialism in Hitler's Germany. But the pathological satisfaction of the need to belong represented by Naziism is nothing more than the result of offering an extreme solution to the need for membership to people under severe threat and desperate for *any* sense of belonging—something we have not fully understood where things like radical Muslim fundamentalism are concerned. So the need to belong is clearly situated at the heart of human satisfaction, especially social satisfaction, and its satisfaction, impoverishment and/or manipulation can have a powerful influence on individuals and groups—even societies—as a whole. Which brings us to the question of the sense of belonging in Western democracies.

One need not belabor the voluminous sociological and social psychological work done in the last century on alienation and anomie to know that, especially in the United States, but increasingly in other Western—and even some non-Western—industrial democracies, the individual sense of belonging has become threadbare and the larger sense of social solidarity has not fared any better. In the US, still a relatively new, if aging, society, where shedding of one's previous ethnic background was almost a requirement for success and integration of newly-arrived immigrants, social solidarity was largely based on the drive to succeed in the eighteenth and nineteenth centuries, and the drive to achieve affluence in the twentieth. But the proliferation of everything from nativist movements to self-development techniques and cults speaks loudly of the absence of a sense of real belonging of the kind that once existed in the ethnic neighborhoods of nineteenth century American cities like Boston, New

York, Chicago and San Francisco, let alone in "the old country" which has been left behind. Even among a group like African-Americans, wherein a sense of belonging-through-exclusion might have once provided a strong sense of solidarity, the existence of gangs with strong ties of self-identification has, at least from the time of Malcolm X's youth, offered a different mode of belonging—and, Maslow would add, a measure of self-esteem.

But even at the level of the everyday, many Americans would have to admit that their sense of belonging is often based on ephemera: "lifestyle" choices from hip-hop to cowboy; "fan" attachments, from music to television; recreation choices, from skateboarding to golf; and the infinity of small things, like nods (real or imagined) to others who drive the same make, model and color of car. In and of themselves, most of these kinds of feelings membership in a group are harmless. The problem comes when they represent the primary, even the exclusive means of satisfying our sense of belonging. And the shift towards other ways of expressing the need to belong that really amount to means of exclusion—the new nativist, anti-immigration groups, many fundamentalist sects—or to groups which establish membership by means of opposition to "the direction we're heading", suggests that our need to belong is seriously, perhaps even dangerously, unsatisfied.

In other Western democracies, some semblance of the old order of belonging still exists for many, their cultures being older and less loosely woven than the American. But it is a fact of modern life that consumer culture erodes the old traditions and replaces them with thinner, much less substantial practices. That the French dedication to fine food and cooking, once almost religious in its intensity, has begun to give way to fast food culture in the shape of such things as McDonald's (*McDou*) and shops dedicated exclusively to prepared frozen dinners (*surgelés*) is one small but very telling example of the way in which, for all their denial of the fact, Europeans have followed the consumerist path first tread by America. Perhaps even more telling is the extent to which the traditional cultures of the former Soviet bloc countries, which had, ironically, been preserved by the role old practices had played as quiet gestures of resistance to communism, have now been almost gleefully shed in the scramble to achieve affluence—which itself is largely represented by participation in increasingly conspicuous consumption.

Even in high context cultures such as Japan and South Korea, where the onset of affluence has been embraced unreservedly, one finds such things as rates of suicide among the highest in the world, attesting to the fact that the tension between the demands of membership in the culture and those of consumer living are creating unbearable stresses on the individual—and by extension on society as a whole. And while most developing countries still have their cultures and traditions in place, creating a much more powerful sense of belonging than exists in the majority of Western democracies, the arrival of affluence among a special few in the population has often created deep rich-poor rifts among peoples who would otherwise feel deeply related, giving rise to (or sometimes amplifying a previously existing) us-them divisions. And, as we have seen, the power of the symbols of consumer culture has penetrated the slum cities and the tribal outposts of virtually every country in the developing world.

We've only covered the first foundations of Maslow's pyramid and we can see already that, if we use his model as a gauge for how well humankind has, at the macro level, achieved the things we all need individually, at the micro level, the balance sheet is not good. And if we take the model a step further up the pyramid, to the level of the need for self-esteem and the esteem of others, the result is, predictably, little better. Self-esteem in the Western industrial democracies of the twenty-first century is painfully hard to come by, whether one talks of the individual or of the society to which he or she belongs. While an individual in these societies may feel some amount of justifiable pride in, say, doing one's job, raising a family, even going to a place of worship, in the broader scheme of things—the vast panorama of developments and trends that wash around us like tides—even those who feel such pride may feel as though they live on small, isolated, and not always very secure islands. With divorce at roughly 50% in most of these countries, even a satisfying marriage and family life can make one feel set apart, blessed but not typical, and the overwhelming statistical realities can create a sense of unease at what might lie ahead. The situation has not been helped by an alleged increase in the standard of living which actually requires most families to generate two incomes—nor are things made any better by the frequent economic upheavals which remind everyone of their relative susceptibility to changing economic winds.

Throughout the industrial West, political alienation, often ignored as a measure of self-esteem, is at an all-time high, and the impact on the individual has been significant: with so little to admire in politics, the personal satisfaction one might normally expect to feel from such things as the mere act of voting is cut off. Where a generation or two ago voters could draw satisfaction from voting for an FDR, a Churchill or a JFK, could even see these figures as public role models, that avenue is for the most part closed. Moreover, the often strident tenor of political discourse suggests the level of frustration many feel with regards to politics; simplistic solutions based on manipulation of sometimes base emotions—about which there will be more to say later—speak loudly to the pervasive sense that politics provides a means of venting resentment, not a source of satisfaction.

And when we deal with the question of the esteem of others, we find not simply the lack of that esteem, but the lack of sufficient means by which to measure whether we enjoy it. Here again, the emphasis on material wealth that has been the natural tendency of the West—and now of other regions as well—is at least partly to blame. In the absence of strong traditional means of gauging the character of one's fellows, as tends to be the situation in the US, or in the face of the decline of those traditions where they do exist, material achievement is the fallback upon which many people rely. Moreover, given that the West's level of material wealth is relatively high and somewhat uniform (though always plagued with troublingly uneven distribution, increasingly so in recent decades), mere "success" is not a sufficient criterion for esteeming one's fellows. To afford us a more highly articulated and (at least superficially) nuanced means of doing so, we turn to the "badges" provided by consumer culture, from designer clothing to travel destinations—or, that ubiquitous measure now made tawdry by the electronic media, fame. Needless to say, these are poor substitutes for the once-powerful measure provided in more traditional society by the quality of the product a craftsperson would produce, the attention a story-teller could command, or the leadership qualities evident in an orator.

Put simply, our condition in the world as we know it, when measured by a known and respected set of measurements of quality of life like Maslow's, is mediocre at best. Those lucky enough to have been born into, or into proximity of, one of the societies which boast a high degree of economic development, while they are afforded a not insignificant modicum of freedom from want that most hominids who have lived on the planet during the last half-million years would have welcomed, do not enjoy what their aspirations might lead them to expect. The rest—the large majority of humankind—may enjoy certain kinds of qualitative benefits attached to the more traditional cultural contexts in which they find themselves, but they may also live in conditions so apalling as to be unimaginable to those in more developed economies; and they often live adjacent to a yawning gulf that could consume them in little more than an instant.

In one sense, what we've said so far is not new. For anyone with a social conscience, from those who follow benevolent religious precepts to those who feel an existential "there but for fortune go I", the environment is full of evidence that things are ... well, as they are. But there are two ways in which this analysis may be said to differ from the many critiques made by progressive thinkers now and for generations past.

To begin with, what we've said so far is built on more than a foundation of moral exhortation or shaming critique. That fact is important because all too often the weight of moral exhortation can be crushing to those who, like most of us, feel powerlessness as one of the defining features of modern life. A consequence of political alienation and disenfranchisement, the magnitude of the complexity of the world in which we live, and the extremes to which the "haves" have become separated from the "have-nots", powerlessness can be profoundly demoralizing, and critique based on such things as liberal guilt can simply, however unintentionally, contribute to the process of that demoralization. Moreover, for better or for worse, moral exhortation can draw attention to the plight of those suffering from injustice and lack of equity in a way that makes political action—or any action—a one-way street: the haves must act on behalf of the have-nots. Since those in affluent societies often do not enjoy the sense of well-being that one naturally associates with their privileged economic status, their subliminal re-action to moral exhortation may be "What about me?"—and un-derstandably so, since the level of satisfaction they enjoy from their privileged status falls so short of what they have been led to expect. To see the state of the world through the lenses of a model like Maslow's allows us to create a continuum upon which *everyone* can be approximately located and their relative positions and circumstances understood. Everyone's needs are taken into consideration, and action can be consolidated so as to point everyone in the direction of improving their lot. Moral exhortation may be implied, but *true* enlightened self-interest can as easily be invoked.

Secondly, a tool like Maslow's gives us the means to go be-yond critique to real, concrete action plans. One of the prob-lems that has long faced progressive political action is the fact that its emphasis has historically been placed on social justice, on "righting wrongs" created by everything from ancient preju-dices to modern opportunism, and a considerable amount of effort has always been expended on extending opportunities to the disenfranchised. However, in an era in which much social injustice has been ameliorated—again, taken relatively, in pro-portion to what has existed in the past and what exists in other parts of the world—progressives in Western democracies really have only two choices: to continue to fly the banner of righting wrongs, which in so many cases runs the risk of seeming tired and outdated, or acknowledging that what remains is not a cru-sade so much as a need to expand a beach head exponentially—no small task, but one which requires taking stock of one's suc-cesses as much as issuing stirring calls to action.

The left, especially in America, has never sufficiently taken credit for its successes, but it should be clear to anyone who scans the landscape of modern industrial societies that dramatic progress has been made on many of the problems of social injustice such as universal suffrage, labor rights, racism and human rights which were pressing only a century ago. A fear of resting on our laurels has kept many progressives from drawing the deeper satisfaction their accomplishments should afford them—when that satisfaction represents the key to expanding the progressive focus and unlocking the energies which are vital to beginning a new phase of social action.

In societies of affluence such as the US, Canada, the EU, and Japan, progressive thinking needs to embrace what might be called "higher order" concerns of the kind that, to members of societies which are still developing, may seem some form of luxury, or even self-indulgence. Take the question of environmental degradation. Until the second half of the twentieth century, it was easy to ignore, or even to applaud, humankind's effect on the environment. Neither the acceleration of technological change nor the fragility of the environment were sufficiently appreciated or understood for the West, which was largely responsible for the acceleration, to realize that there might be limits to what the planet could absorb let alone the possibility that we might be approaching those limits. Before the twentieth century, means and materials were the primary concern for production of everything from food to art; neither waste nor knock-on environmental effects got much, if any, attention—even when, say in nineteenth century London, the effects were near-catastrophic. The realization that limits had to be recognized involved a higher order consideration: one that required a larger view that had not previously even existed. Today, over a half century since this realization began to dawn on us (Rachael Carson's *The Silent Spring* might well be seen as the first light of that dawn in America), the West is still struggling to absorb the magnitude of this higher order consideration and

Dan Shanahan

integrate it into its world view. And, needless to say, developing countries struggling to establish some semblance of what the Western industrial democracies consider normality often either feel less urgency about the environmental costs of development or resent the fact that environmental concerns are coming to the fore after the West has achieved affluence but before they themselves have been able to.

Little of any of this would have made sense to someone a mere century ago—in some cases, even a half century ago. But the environmental costs of development, and the limits they have revealed about how much and how fast development can proceed, have opened the door to whole new levels of consideration about how to judge action plans. Successful growth, something that has weighed heavily in the calculus of our well-being at least since the beginnings of civilization, has been superceded by something we haven't even yet coined a phrase for: "planet resource management" is one characterization which, while it risks being tainted by overtones of New Age utopianism, says it as well as anything.

But the higher order considerations that have begun to attract our attention, and which have proliferated so quickly that our lack of a unifying overview of them often allows them obscure our vision, are hardly limited to "hard" questions like environmental degradation. On the contrary, the psychological discontents that a close look at consumer culture reveals are just such higher order problems. When seen in the light of some of the far more desperate circumstances that exist in developing societies, they may take on the appearance of marginal concerns, even luxuries. But they are not. In fact, such seemingly inconsequential concerns—again, inconsequential when seen in light of the starvation, disease, war, and social desperation that exists in so many parts of the globe—as "job

54

satisfaction", political disaffection, increasing divorce rates or decline in civil society, to name a few, are real on several counts: they plague the very populations which, by virtue of the affluence they enjoy, can look at the global picture more clearly; they may disincline those populations from taking action because of the demoralization they spread; and, most importantly, *they can be said to unify those in the affluent societies with those in the non-affluent societies.*

In the global outrage that followed the September 11 attacks, and in the volumes of analysis that have appeared since, explanations for the attacks and for the rise of terrorism, especially acts undertaken by fundamentalist groups, have ranged from vapid, self-serving remarks about how the terrorists "hate us for our freedom" to analyses based on conflicts of civilizations, cultures and religions. Many (myself included) turned to books like Dostoevsky's *The Possessed* for some deeper understanding of the kind of mind that must lay behind such avowedly murderous acts. But in the end, most analyses tend to start, however latently, from some sort of us/them dichotomy: "they" are the perpetrators of the terror, "we" are the targets. And the assumption is that "they" have a different perspective—Islamic, Arabic, neo-Marxist, Maoist in some cases, or simply barbaric—from "us".

In fact, a far better understanding of fundamentalist terrorism—of *all* kinds, from Islamic fundamentalists attacking "the West", to fundamentalist Christians shooting doctors who perform abortion, to pseudo-libertarians attacking forestry agents and government buildings—emerges if we recognize that all these groups see themselves as under threat and that the threats they perceive arise from the very changes which accompanied affluence in the industrial democracies, ultimately leaving the affluent less than satisfied with their lot. Much has been made by commentators on the right of the fact that the leaders of a group like al Quaeda, far from being impoverished, were often from very wealthy families: this, they claimed, gave the lie to the notion that their acts reflected the have/have not gap which exists between the Islamic masses and the affluent West. But the fact that someone comes from a wealthy family does not preclude him or her having deep doubts about the direction taken by their society; indeed, in almost any society the wealthy are often more likely to uphold conservative values than the poor. Small wonder, then, that conservative, educated—and often religious—members of Islamic societies felt greater and greater anxiety over the waves of Westernization they have seen breaking over their cultures in the last several decades. The handwriting has been on the wall for some time: Western materialism, consumerism and, in their eyes, decadence, is like a cancer that has been slowly destroying what they see as the healthy tissue of their traditional practices and beliefs, religious and cultural. In the face of Western unconcern over the way in which their worlds have been undermined, they took matters into their own hands. However rarefied their logic, brutal their intent or extreme their view, what they have set out to do is not so mysterious.

So too the case of others whose fundamentalism may be religious or may simply reflect the desire to return to a less complicated or more moral time, however illusionary the simplicity or morality of past times may actually be. Libertarians who attack government personnel and installations, abortion opponents who attack doctors, are not unlike al Quaeda in that their core belief involves the conviction that modern life has infringed on fundamental features of the world they want to see protected, upheld and preserved. Moreover, their willingness to take radically extreme measures in defense of their beliefs is a measure of their desperation, of the degree to which they feel threatened by the changes that have swamped their lives. Nor, it must be said, are any of these radical extremists that different from the individuals who, in nations as diverse as the US, Germany, Sweden, Brazil and China, feel themselves pushed to such extremes by the stresses of modern life that they turn on colleagues, school children or mere passersby with the same murderous intent. Each of these groups has its own "take", its own logic which explains their anger and their frustration (though in the last case it may border on the completely irrational); but each of them has simply succumbed to lashing out at the forces they hold responsible for the stresses they feel—stresses which, ultimately, we all feel, but which some may feel less, or be better at coping with, than others.

In other words, we all feel the impact of forces—usually impersonal forces that can be easier to contend with if we give them a face, a name or an affiliation—which have changed the world we thought we knew and have forced us to adjust. Whether the change involves the loss of a kindler, simpler world we believe once existed, or the very real ravaging of the ancient cultures and traditions that have been part of our societies for centuries, we find satisfaction—a sense of stability and security, a sense of belonging to a group we value, self-esteem and the esteem of others—harder to find. Yet very clearly, *these are higher order considerations.* They go beyond the most basic considerations of food, clothing and shelter, and our failure to find satisfaction in relation to them undermines our belief in the value of the way we live our lives. And the fact that they have impact on us all, rich and poor, affluent and developing, discontent or desperate is, paradoxically, a unifying element in the experience of most who exist on the planet today. To be sure, the consequences of the changes we have experienced may vary in magnitudes that make the extremes seem separated by an infinity of distance: the single mother in Soweto who sees her children's attention galvanized by Nikes and hip-hop while she can barely scrape together the means to support them inhabits a world far removed from the single mother in suburban America who competes with television and the internet as she tries to raise children with a true appreciation of the values she holds dear. But both face the reality of stresses unknown to people who occupied analogous positions in their societies a century ago. And in both cases, we are looking at problems that involve higher order considerations—*quality of life* considerations that cannot be measured quantitatively.

So progressive political thinking faces a challenge—indeed, a whole set of challenges—which did not even exist in the world of Herbert Croly and the progressives of his age. First, a complete reorientation of thinking away from the notion that material well-being is the ultimate goal of political action must take place: material well-being of a kind probably unimaginable to people of Croly's time has been established for the majority of those living in Western industrialized countries; what now needs to be addressed is the *quality* of life led by those who have achieved that well-being. Second, everything—*everything*, from dire poverty to high finance—has connections with everything else on a global scale. Degrees of interconnectedness, interdependency and the obligation to pay close attention to these links may differ from case to case; but our world is like a giant concave bowl with marbles covering the bottom: move one marble, and it has consequences for all the other marbles, individually and as a whole. Thus progressive thinking must include global questions such as poverty and development within the very structure of its reorientation, not as a function of liberal guilt, *noblesse oblige* or the vestiges of "white man's burden" imperialism, but as part of an action program which makes human satisfaction the foundation goal.

Finally, while it would be easy to imagine that quality of life is a concern restricted to societies of affluence and basics of life to societies still in development, this is a false notion and one that violates the realities that require a reorientation. Progressive political thinking must recognize that those in developing countries confront many of the quality of life concerns of those in affluent societies, albeit in sometimes disguised form; and while in some respects the persistence of elements of traditional society, like the extended family, may provide something of a cushion against the stresses of modern life, the existence of both, side by side, one gradually superceding the other, creates additional stresses in and of itself. Moreover, development in emergent economies must be allowed to benefit from the wisdom produced by the mistakes of those countries which have achieved affluence, both in "hard" terms, as with respect to the environment, and in more elusive matters, like the impact of over-commercialization. At bottom, progressive political thinking must recognize the fundamental unity of basic human needs and higher order concerns, and it must develop action plans which emphasize the common, if differing, ground shared by "haves" and "have-nots" as the world begins to marshal its resources in the fully globalized environment now taking shape.

Such a reorientation is a tall order. However, there is an additional contingency to be addressed that, while it complicates our work in some respects, provides a means and a guide for proceeding without the need of an ideological blueprint. For if anything is requisite to reorienting progressive political thinking, it is the need for discussion and dialogue about these matters. It is the question of how that discussion can take place, how that dialogue can be established—and the formidable obstacles both face—that we turn to next.

IV

Discussions take place in an environment, dialogue can only be established in a context—and sadly, the political context in America, while it may represent an extreme, is not uncharacteristic of contexts in many countries: adversarial divisions, some of them superficial, but many deeply rooted in social and cultural conflicts of long standing, threaten to make true discussion and dialogue impossible. In the US, the sometimes viral social discords of the 1960s left a legacy we now most frequently characterize as the red state-blue state division: red states leaning towards a conservative political ideology, blue states towards a liberal one. The conservative-liberal division itself is almost as old as politics, and probably represents some guarantee that politics will not veer off too radically in one direction or the other. But what is increasingly disturbing about the red-blue split as it exists in the US—and as it reflects analogous developing splits in other industrial democracies—is the extent to which it has become an almost paralyzing factionalism in day to day politics. The entrenched nature of the positions taken by each side, whether on taxes, growth of government, abortion, sexual preference, family values, or the myriad of other hot-button issues that have plagued the country for decades. So deeply entrenched are the positions on so many issues, discussion seems almost to have ground to a halt, dialogue becomes an impossibility.

Let's begin by clarifying those two words. By discussion, I mean the kind of back-and-forth give-and-take that takes place when there is an issue at hand that must be aired and a variety of opinions to be expressed about it. A community may want to decide about building a new school; there will be arguments for and against, they will be aired over time and, in the best of cases, a consensus will emerge. But dialogue is something more. In a real dialogue, there is a basic agreement on at least one thing: the matter at hand is of importance and must be dealt with, perhaps urgently, but from a position of common ground and mutual respect. Partners in the dialogue may disagree, strongly perhaps, about what kind of action needs to be taken, but they agree that something must be done and they try to use that agreement as the basis for including aspects of all points of view in a solution. The negotiations surrounding the Cuban Missile Crisis in 1962, wherein the two superpowers' fear of the prospect of mutual annihilation allowed them to back out of the corner in which they found themselves, had strong elements of dialogue.

Dialogue seems to have all but disappeared from national politics in America, and discussion has fared little better. While there is sometimes agreement on the importance of an issue—the need for health care reform in the 2009–10 debate, for instance—so different are the perspectives that rhetorical attacks, sound-bite catch phrases, name calling and outright misrepresentation (admittedly, the most gratuitous of these originating on the political right) replaced anything like discussion, let alone dialogue. There are those progressives who would respond to the more egregious of the right's use of rhetorical attacks by recasting the progressive message, pointing out that phrases like "death tax" and "partial birth abortions" resonate with certain public fears and evoke resistance to necessary change and that progressives must find similar resonating catch-words. There is much to be said for this kind of intelligent rebranding of the progressive message; however, it merely fuels the fires that already consume what little oxygen there may be to feed genuine discussion and dialogue. What progressives need is a deeper understanding of the dynamic that underlies the entrenchment that has taken place on the right; reestablishing the grounds for dialogue and discussion is unlikely to come from that end of the political spectrum, and understanding why provides a basis for a progressive appeal to those who may be fooled by the increasingly hysterical characterizations of the right.

Let's start with Sarah Palin.

During the headier days of the '08 campaign, when the world of presidential politics had been surprised by the nomination of Sarah Palin as John McCain's Republican running mate, and pundits scrambled to explain, interpret, or otherwise come to terms with what seemed, at best, a bizarre selection, George Lakoff wrote a piece which attempted to demonstrate the tactical wisdom of McCain's choice.[5] Lakoff's argument was, in essence, that because metaphors dominate the way we think, Palin would appeal to one of the "foundation metaphors" of the nation generally and conservatives especially: the family. Everything else, Lakoff said—the "pro-life" stance, abstinence-only attitudes, tough love for criminals, etc.—followed naturally

5   http://www.buzzflash.com/articles/articles/contributors/1728

63

from this foundation metaphor, making Palin a powerful addition to the Republican ticket.

I know Lakoff's academic research and have used it frequently in my own. I respect him and his work a great deal and think his explanation was helpful as far as it went. But, while it offers an explanation that tries to go beneath the surface of appearances—where, all too often in American politics of the last forty years, "truth" and "falsehood" appear pitted against one another in a do-or-die battle (another metaphor Lakoff might have pointed to)—the "family as foundation metaphor" doesn't really go far enough toward explaining "the Palin phenomenon", particularly in her emergence as a spokesperson for the extreme right since the election. While appealing to foundation metaphors like the family could never hurt a candidate, Palin's rag-tag family group had little that could compete with the Obamas, their obviously healthy marriage, two charming daughters, and the ancestral checkerboard that the family represented. At best, the match-up would have been a draw. But the truth is that Palin invigorated feelings in both camps that went far beyond the mere appeal to family. Palin was, indeed, a phenomenon, and one has to go deeper than the workings of foundation metaphors to understand why.

Lakoff[6] has ably shown that metaphors permeate, not only our language, but the very nature of our perceptions. We find our language littered with them—remarks (like "littered with") that we never intend to be taken literally, but which rely on metaphorical connections our listeners will understand, even if only subliminally. We are capable of locomotion, so we commonly say things (like "I don't follow your logic") that are based on what "locomotors" use: paths. We can perceive inside and outside, so

6   Along with Mark Johnson, Mark Turner, Zoltan Kovacses and others.

we use container metaphors: "The verdict filled him with rage". We rely a lot on organs of sight called "eyes", so we say things like "I see your point". And so on. Lakoff has used these insights to great effect analyzing how the conservative wing of the Republican Party has cast its message in metaphorical terms so as to engage its audience both explicitly and implicitly.

But metaphors rely on language, whether in the form of speech, body language, images, or any of the other forms that we use daily and that have become part of the political process. We can't refer to a government or a nation as "the ship of state" without talking, writing, signing, or perhaps miming in some way that is genuinely linguistic. And though from Plato through Sartre we have tended to see language as one of our rational cognitive functions, we are beginning to understand that *language has emotional roots*. Uncovering those roots is a complex job that we have only just begun,[7] but using those roots is one of the ways in which metaphor evokes and amplifies the power of what we are trying to say.

The greater the emotional power a metaphor has, the better it works. If I tell you my electrical service has been "discontinued", it carries less impact than if I say it has been "cut"— even though the latter is a metaphorical expression: no actual physical cutting has taken place. So too with political discourse. When JFK talked of the "New Frontier", he was evoking powerful associations with the American past which, in part via their then-currency in film and television, helped to convince the electorate that America was "boldly going forth" to achieve a new greatness. When Ronald Reagan spoke of "an evil empire", he was evoking feelings associated with everything from

7   I tried to help that process along in *Language, Feeling and the Brain: The Evocative Vector* (New Brunswick: Transaction Publishers, 2007).

65

Puritan notions of good and evil to Lukasian Death Stars. And Jimmy Carter, who otherwise did much to reintroduce religion into American politics, inexplicably missed a chance to energize the electorate in the fight to conserve energy by failing to introduce the obvious, but very powerful, parallel that existed between the oil crises of the 70s and the Biblical story of Joseph's interpretation of Pharoh's dreams. (In that case, Carter failed on a number of levels, choosing an improbable metaphor for energy conservation, "war", and stating it as a logical "equivalent", rather than evoking the power of a real metaphor, like "a crusade against wasteful consumption".)

Metaphor is a mode of expression that uses comparison to evoke a bit of the mythological, even the magical power of language. But myths and metaphors are only as powerful as the associations they draw upon—and the emotions that fuel those associations. And this is where Lakoff's explanation of "the Palin phenomenon" falls short. Evoking family metaphors couldn't have saved Michael Dukakis—or Jimmy Carter, who had homespun Amy to go up against Ronald Reagan's very non-typical, Hollywood progeny. Nor did JFK have to invoke the family metaphor to garner the votes in the midst of America's great Baby Boom: he rode the crest of a much more powerful wave of post-War American triumphalism, faith in technology and youthful "vigor"—all powerful feelings that were already present in the contemporary American consciousness, waiting for the right combination of images and messages to evoke them. Feelings, the things that candidates evoke consciously (like the saccharine nostalgia of Reagan's "Morning in America" motif) and subliminally (the "aw shucks", regular guy appeal of George W. Bush) constitute much of the real currency of political images and messages. And to understand Sarah Palin's appeal, you have to look more carefully at the emotions she evoked.

Some attributed Palin's appeal to the strong American tradition of anti-intellectualism so aptly portrayed by Richard Hofstadter (ironically, from a fairly conservative viewpoint), and there is certainly more than a small amount of truth in that analysis. Americans have always liked to see themselves as no-nonsense, New England farmers spouting pithy (metaphorical) remarks such as "If it walks like a duck, talks like a duck, and acts like a duck, it must be a duck". Palin, they say, appealed to Americans who want to "cut through the long-winded garbage" (one can easily imagine those very words coming from her at a campaign rally) and she clearly helped give vent to the frustrations of many who would like to think that complex ideas are nothing more than high-IQ clutter. For that portion of the electorate, political choices are a lot simpler than policy wonks and intellectuals make them sound; we need to get back to basics, they say. Ronald Reagan evoked those feelings throughout his presidency (and his governorship, for those of us who experienced it first hand), and his legacy has been to provide a touchstone for all those who feel that government is an obstacle, rather than an aid, to our lives.

But Palin's appeal drew on more powerful emotions than mere skepticism about intellectuals and ideas, and in so doing evoked a set of feelings with far graver import for a democracy. It was easy at first to be confused, or even bemused, by Palin's naive housewife persona, the awe and even awkwardness she first displayed in the face of the role she'd been chosen to play. But she showed her true colors when, in her acceptance speech in the Twin Cities, Palin made her now-famous references to herself as a "hockey mom" and a "pit bull". Speaking in a code that was secret to no one in contemporary America, Palin was contrasting "hockey moms" with "soccer moms": the former drive pickups, not Volvos; they drink cups of "Jo", not lattés;

67

they eat caribou, not tofu; they get their news from the television, not the print media; and so on. Moreover, and more importantly, they have chosen their moniker as a kind of "in your face" (and virulently anti-intellectual) response to the snobby, sophisticated, "liberals" they despise.

Strong word, "despise". But it was the right one if you listened to the underlying—and highly emotional—tone of Palin's speech. Contempt for intellectuals and the Left virtually dripped from her words when she compared herself and other hockey moms to pit bulls—the trophy pet of the urban gang and the neo-Nazi. And the same tone infused her remarks about the media and serving "the American people". Indeed, that tone was the hallmark—and the clarion call—of most of her acceptance speech. Whatever advantage her status as a representative of the family foundation metaphor might have been, this was anything but a family mom speaking, unless you redefine motherhood as having some deep connection with Dirty Harry. This was not June Lockhart, Donna Reed, or any of the other mothers we so readily—and often naively—associate with the myth of "the American family". This was a snarling attack dog, full of spittle and spite, ready to spring, barely held back by the leash of appearing on national television. And *that's* what the excitement was all about—at least among what the Republicans then saw as the "core" constituency McCain couldn't guarantee he could deliver. That's what made the choice of Palin over, say, Governor Mike Huckabee, work. She invoked and invigorated feelings, not only of frustration, but of deep animosity towards an "enemy"—"liberals"—and legitimized those feelings as a basis for political action, saying, in effect, "Tempered thought is a con: we know what's right; let's clear the bums out who stand in our way".

There *is* a kind of foundation metaphor here, and a decidedly American one, but it's not family. It's the Wild West and Dodge

City. (Camille Paglia called Palin a kind of Annie Oakley.) It's "go in and clean up the town" John Waynism. And worse. It's Ronald Reagan on crystal, it's Charlton Heston's "cold, dead hands" come back to life gripping an assault rifle. And, of course, all in the name of things like "American values".

There's nothing new about this: Americans have always wanted to see themselves as "the good guys" who demonstrate to the world how things really should be. That, in fact, may be their ultimate foundation metaphor: the Puritans fleeing decadent Europe (*i.e.* England, Spain, the Papacy, etc.—everything Donald Rumsfeld evoked when he referred to "Old Europe") to start over again. (And the left has not been immune from similar self-serving oversimplifications, 60s slogans like "You're either part of the problem or part of the solution" being prime examples.) But the real calculus which explains the Palin "phenomenon" is the not the metaphor, but the emotions which the metaphor is used to evoke. And clearly, those emotions are 1) resentment, and 2) resentment's pit bull cousin, revenge.

In every one of Palin's pronouncements on "cleaning up Washington" or "bringing change to politics" the foundation emotion was resentment, and in this she followed a long tradition of the disenfranchised on both sides of the political spectrum that goes back through Reagan and George Wallace at least to Andrew Jackson. (In ,68, a working class family in my neighborhood had RFK posters and bumper stickers prominently displayed until Bobby was shot. Within two days, they had been replaced with twice as many "Wallace for President" signs.) People who feel disenfranchised become resentful, and galvanizing that resentment can produce a lot of political capital for those who are opportunistic enough to do so. The dominance of the Democratic Party in the South from 1865 to 1968, a consequence of the South's deeply felt resentment over Reconstruction, is one of the most formidable examples in American history. But even graver examples litter European history, at least until the catastrophic consequences of galvanizing resentment gave them World War II and the Holocaust—and an equally grave pause about how they conducted their political lives.

What was, and continues to be troubling about the Palin "phenomenon" was the degree to which it openly, and even gleefully, pits resentment against measured judgment, offering the possibility of revenge as the reward for fighting liberals. Her appeal has been a slightly more polite form of the Charles Bronson film formula: whip up the "I've had it up to here" feelings to a fever pitch, and let them explode into an electoral land (or mud) slide. "Join me and we'll tar and feather the varmints and run them out of town on a rail", is the message. And abandonment of anything resembling reasoned discussion, let alone dialogue, is its hallmark.[8]

But perhaps the best way to see how much the Palin phenomenon relied on raw, and very resentful, emotions is to see how the winning side did not. No one can say that Barack Obama's campaign avoided emotional appeal. Everything about Obama, from his winning smile to his "superstar" status to the "Yes We Can" chant, beamed with the good feelings generated by his candidacy. But notice how different the word "beamed" is from any word or phrase one would choose to characterize the feelings evoked by the Palin phenomenon. Clearly, there was what some might call a kind of "moral uplift" to the feelings generated by the Obama campaign—not least because the serious candidacy

---

8   Clearly, the Tea Party movement, allegedly grass root populism, but in fact heavily financed by the right wing Koch brothers' millions, has become the organized manifestation of the resentment embodied in Palin's message.

of an African American helped to right moral wrongs that were centuries old in America. But in and of themselves, emotions that provide some sort of "uplift" are not necessarily, in and of themselves, enough. Think again of the saccharine, and ultimately very shallow appeal of the "Morning in America" campaign; think too about how much the "New Frontier" attitude contributed to things like growing American involvement in Vietnam. More than uplift is required if a campaign—or a program for political action—is to encourage discussion and dialogue and lead the way to a focus on the higher order considerations that must be included in any progressive political action plan. And it was here, perhaps, that the distinctions between the Obama and the Palin phenomena were most glaring.

In the place of resentment, the Obama campaign built on feelings that arose from notions of inclusion, cooperation, and mutual respect. Moreover, those feelings were perceived, rightly in my estimation, as deeply felt by the candidate. Nothing could have been more illustrative of the willingness of the candidate to see things from the other side's point of view than the briefly infamous episode in San Francisco where Obama was heard to say that many right-to-lifers and gun rights supporters held onto their beliefs so tenaciously because so much else had been taken away from them. While right wing pundits tried to make the remark out to be an insult to the intelligence of the anti-abortion and gun lobbies, it was difficult for any but the most resentful—or the most calculating—to ignore the fact that the remark was made as an expression of feelings of concern: concern about political discourse in America, concern about achieving real dialogue among political viewpoints, and concern about generating feelings of inclusion among those who felt themselves and their values under attack. In fact, time and again candidate Obama demonstrated his ability and his willingness to exhibit feelings of generosity, good will and empathy for all segments of the American population. What's more, there is no doubt that the evocation of those feelings helped him to a remarkably ecumenical victory in what had been, up until then, a notoriously parochial electorate.

If there is a moral or a lesson to be drawn from the 2008 campaign it is that it is not just the metaphors you use, the myths you build on or even whether or not you evoke emotions: everyone does. The "phenomenon phenomena" are best understood in light of the quality of the emotions they evoke. In the end, the emotions evoked by a political campaign, a political party or a political philosophy will reveal a great deal about the *real* agenda that underlies the sound bites, the images and the rhetoric. Of course, the need for wise policy, effective management and imagination cannot be ignored. Though the Bush administration managed to evoke and sustain emotions of fear and determination that "we don't get fooled again", its failure to chose the right venue for confronting terrorism (the war in Iraq), to handle non-political problems effectively (Katrina) and to find new ways of dealing with old problems (health care, financial regulation, the Middle East, etc., etc., etc.) guaranteed it would lose the support even of many who shared the feelings it played upon.

But in looking at the way emotions, myths and metaphors influence political messages—and their messengers—we cannot ignore two important facts of political life. First, not all political figures have that special quality—for many years we called it "charisma"—which allows them to communicate powerfully with their audience. A rare few do: FDR, Churchill, JFK, Martin Luther King. Some less magnetic political leaders rise to the moment from time to time, assuming "the bully pulpit" perhaps, and lifting political discourse out of the humdrum of everyday life. But oddly, political success, even success that is built on integrity and vision, does not necessarily require skills of com-munication commensurate with the magnitude and complexity of the problems that constitute everyday, as well as momentous, politics. That simple, inescapable fact leads us to another: to substitute for real discussions about real problems and real op-tions for solving them, it is often the case that politicians will resort to harangue, hyperbole—and worse. There is a little of the first two almost any political discussion; however the dan-ger comes when, for lack of the ability (or the desire) to analyze problems in a measured and thoughtful way, any hope of real discussion is displaced by the willingness to play to baser emo-tions. Here again, Ronald Reagan was a master of disguising the extent to which his "message" was built on sentiments of frus-tration and resentment, veiling them with techniques gleaned from his days in film and on television, and earning the title "the great communicator" on the basis of his ability to ring the bell of middle-class resentment while appearing to speak rea-sonably and without artifice. And Reagan can be credited with ushering in a whole new era in which the evocation of senti-ments like resentment—once consigned to the likes of Father Coughlin, Joe McCarthy and George Wallace—was considered respectable. The Tea Party is his heir.

The difficult question for the left is how, in the absence of an FDR or a JFK, to counter the effect of this appeal to very power-ful baser emotions and at the same time to foster discussion and dialogue. I can see only one answer: *gravitas.*

If there is a figure who, in my lifetime, could command respect, be inclusive, be judicious and avoid raising passions beyond what was appropriate to the matters at hand, it was Bar-bara Jordan. Congresswoman Jordan was, for many of us, the figure who first gave rise to the hope that both a woman and an African American could occupy the White House—this long before Barack Obama or Hillary Clinton had even appeared on the political scene. Had she lived to achieve her potential, she would have represented much of what is so sorely missing from American political discourse today. Some of that was a function of her personality, though I suspect we would have had to invent another word than "charisma" to identify the special something in her character that carried with it a seriousness appropriate to modern democratic discussion and dialogue. But I would argue that such seriousness is not in the personality of the political figure him or herself, but *in the way he or she addresses themselves to the problems that face the body politic.*

Perhaps the best recent example of such seriousness was the speech on race that Barack Obama gave in response to the controversy over remarks made by his pastor, Jeremiah Wright. In his speech addressing the anger and resentment reflected in Reverend Wright's remarks about racism in America and the subsequent furor over those remarks, Candidate Obama did what few political operators ever do: he addressed the controversy frontally, peeled away its outer layer to uncover the real forces at work, and called it the way he saw it, "chips fall where they may", and he did so with such insight, clarity and honesty, that the "Wright problem" just went away. Period.

But one of the more remarkable things about the speech was the fact that Obama changed his delivery very little from what he had used in countless previous addresses. He did not become grave or even much more sober than he had been previously. The seriousness he displayed was in his analysis of the matter at hand. Much of that analysis was boiler-plate reflection on the status of African Americans in America—reflection that, in the hands of many liberal critics of contemporary America, could have become admonishing, harsh, even accusatory. But in place of such techniques that, it could be argued, have become so worn and overused that they fall on deaf ears even when the audience is sympathetic, Obama stated the obvious *as obvious*. In speaking of the frustration that many black Americans still feel about their lot, he made his remarks with an implicit "these things we know" in his voice; and he did so with a sense of resignation to the facts as givens, but with a clear underlying message: these are obstacles we face to which we must find solutions.

When he spoke of Wright's remarks, he did not dodge their obvious import, nor attempt to spin them: he acknowledged their harmful acidity; but then he underlined how much a part of the landscape of contemporary America these remarks were by asking whether he should have disowned his white grandparents for the traces of involuntary racism he sometimes saw in them. What's more, he did so with a foot in the camp of many white Americans who, out of a sense of fair play more endemic in the American character than many progressives are willing to recognize, want to see the country move beyond racism. Moreover, like the good community organizer he was, Obama said nothing to inflame the resentments of those who feel affirmative action violates their sense of fair play, those who harbor fears that black advancement will take place at their expense, etc., etc. He may not have convinced any of them that Wright's sentiments were understandable; but by avoiding a moral diatribe, he reassured them that understanding, not making political points, was his goal.

In short candidate Obama treated his audience and his topic seriously enough to deal with the reality of the situation frontally and honestly, without hiding behind diatribe or spin. He did not rely on predictable emotions in the fashion of Sarah Palin and those who find her brand of mindless resentment attractive; he adopted a serious but non-accusatory emotional tone. And in so doing he set himself sufficiently above the fray to demonstrate that he occupied the higher ground. *That* was *gravitas*. Sadly, we have precious little of this honest confrontation with hard realities since candidate Obama became President Obama. But that fact, usually subsumed under the notion that an elected official must represent all the people ("You run from the left/right but you govern from the center".), reveals a sad truth about American political life today—and one which is not unique to American democracy: political leaders often fail to trust the members of the electorate to recognize the truth when it is laid out honestly before them.

There is a deeper question here than whether or not one listens to the polls, to the pundits and to the professional political operatives, and it is not hyperbolic to say that it goes to the very heart of democratic theory and values. The question is, quite simply, do we trust the electorate?

In the age of mass society and mass communication that was born when first there emerged something we could call "the reading public"—and now encompasses virtually everyone with access to a radio, television, or internet connnection—we have come to take for granted the "dumbing down" of communication of all kinds. Television, with its "least common denominator" attitude towards programming has most frequently taken the brunt of the criticism aimed at this tendency. But in fact, the Fleet Street tabloids which predated television by a century and a half indulged in many of the same dumbing-down practices that we have come to associate with the more shabby tendencies of electronic media—most especially the willingness to engage in everything from speculative exaggeration ("sources close to the President have been heard to say") to pandering to the prurient interests of the public (choose your scandal *de jour*).

The point of these practices has been to attract attention, usually with the aim of increasing circulation—and therefore profits—but also with the not infrequent goal of pushing a political agenda. Nor has this been purely the territory of the political opportunists: Nelly Bly, Ida Tarbell, Lincoln Steffens and Upton Sinclair used some of the techniques of the tabloid press to draw attention to matters of vital importance. But the need to draw attention has, especially in an age in which the barrage of information has come to fill the environment like a blizzard of white noise, not only become a fundamental preeoccupation of anyone who attempts to communicate with the public at large, it has spilled over into our notions of how one is to attract the attention of the *electorate*. Without necessarily meaning to (though in an ample number of cases, the intention to do so has been quite clear), the political establishment has come to presume that "attention getting" messages must be crafted if one is to get through the white noise blizzard. And attention-getting, by definition, usually involves some measure of dumbing down— if not a resort to hyperbole and outright hysteria.

There are a number of fallacies at work here in what has become a foundational assumption of politics in virtually every modern democracy, but perhaps the lie they perpetuate is best exposed at the heart of what many people—with only partial justification—see as the source of the problem, commercial television. The conventional wisdom has it that television offers deliberately low-brow and mind-numbing programming (*The Beverly Hillbillies* has always been the target of thinking baby boomers in this respect) in order to insure ratings that will allow it to sell commercial time. But that wisdom ignores the fact that, since television's earliest days, quality programming has done quite well (think of *Playhouse 90* or *The Honeymooners* in the 50s)—and it still does so today. From *Mash* to *Cheers* to

Frasier, from *Hill Street Blues* to *LA Law* to *The West Wing*, programming that reflects high standards of drama and comedy has not only done well, it has frequently swept the boards both in terms of ratings and awards. In other words, the assumption that the public will not respond to quality programming is patently false: on the contrary, programming that is dumbed down rarely has the impact that high quality programming does. (It's worth noting that the same is true of film and—think only of the Beatles—popular music.)

In other words, there is ample evidence at the source to suggest that, even in a "mass" environment, the public can be trusted to respond to quality messages. Put so baldly as this, one wonders that such a remark has to be made at all. Democracy rests on the assumption that, given the opportunity, the people can be discriminating in their choices. But in an age of consumerism and white noise, we have let ourselves slide insidiously toward the opposite set of assumptions: that people respond more to bombast than to bravura, to demagoguery than to dialogue. The right has been almost gleeful in its embrace of those assumptions, using them to justify manipulation of the audience around emotions of resentment and exclusion, as Palin does. For its part, while the left has mostly avoided temptation on this count (excluding such things as Hillary Clinton's and Geraldine Ferraro's half-gaffes about race in 2008), it has done little to counter the tendency.

But how do we construct quality messages? Let me start with an example from the classroom which has surprised even me with the force of its impact on discussion of thing which are "hard to get a handle on". In my course, "Human Relationships in Film", we spend a term looking at how romance, marriage and family, and social relationships are portrayed, with an eye toward providing students with tools (and handles) which will serve them as they try to choose mates, friends, establish families, and so on—a task that ought to be at the center of our educational efforts in any society, but isn't. We begin the course with Zeffirelli's *Romeo and Juliet* and I guide the discussion towards asking, for instance, whether or not the feelings that emerge between the two main characters are "real" love. Later on we read Fromm's *The Art of Loving*; but at this stage in the course I want to elicit the inevitable comments about "true love" that fill the minds and discourses of students in their late teens and early twenties.

Most students will agree that the feelings that exist between Romeo and Juliet constitute something we can call "love" in the elevated (rather than the mundane, Hollywood- and Tin Pan Alley-bound) sense of the word, but they have difficulty saying why. When the difficulty of finding the right words to express their intuitive impressions creates, as it always does, an impasse in the discussion, I suggest two things about the balcony scene that tell us the two lovers' encounter is more than passing infatuation, lust, rebellion against their familes, etc. I say that we're impressed, as an audience, by the *transparency* that both Romeo and Juliet display (R: "there lies more peril in thine eye/ Than in twenty of their swords"; J: "I should have been more strange, I must confess") and by the *discovery* that each experiences: each has found another being with the same feelings, the same fears, the same needs that they have.

When I first landed on the words "transparency" and "discovery" to use in the discussion, it wasn't planned: I was spontaneously trying to dig deep and come up with words that meant what I was trying to express. In the process I landed on words that had been current in my own years as a student, as my friends and I struggled to deal with questions of identity and relationship. But what was remarkable was how quickly the

79

students responded to the the words. While I subsequently give them a passage from Maslow's discussion of what he calls "Being-love" and "Deficiency-love" that characterizes love in much the same way, the passage merely serves as reinforcement: for them, we have staked out the turf we're covering with our own terms, and the ground we cover thereafter is ours.

Political dialogue, if it is to be restablished in America, needs to do the same, and given that the right has become almost addicted to the use of neo-Orwellian terms (death tax, pro-life, etc.) it will be up to the left to introduce meaningful terms into the political discourse. Where to begin? I would suggest that we begin with the terms each side uses to identify itself and its opposition. Terms like right and left are emotionally charged political monikers that do little but emphasize the "sidedness" of what passes for discourse. So too the term "liberal", which has little relationship to what it intends to signify. In fact, perhaps the only contemporary term which offers a reasonably accurate characterization of those it identifies is "conservative". A conservative believes that "new" is not necessarily "better", he or she wants to conserve those things which are best, and to move slowly enough to insure that change does not mean abandoning what is good in favor of what is new or, worse yet, fashionable. And few who value democracy can deny that *there is value and wisdom inherent in conservatism* as we've characterized it here.

In contrast, there are those of us who feel that, to paraphrase Woody Allen, democratic society is like a shark: it has to keep moving through the water to stay alive. As we've seen, transformational movement is the way of the universe, and it has always been the way of societies, particularly as humankind's ability to transform its environment has, in the last two centuries, expanded trigonometrically. Much of that transformation has been beneficial, or at least promises benefits to the whole of

humankind if it is wisely managed, and can therefore be characterized with the term "progress". It seems only right, therefore,
that those of us who recognize the value of everything from
advances in medicine to advances in respect for human rights
should, therefore, call themselves "progressives".

There is also a hidden advantage to using these terms: few
would disagree that there are things to be conserved and progress to be made in the world that we face—that, in fact, all democratic societies stand to gain from a wise blend of progressive
and conservative attitudes. So to call the opposition by a name
that carries with it the implication that its view has a place in
the work that faces us is, by definition, *to reestablish the basis
for true political dialogue*. Here again, Barack Obama, candidate,
provided a poignant illustration of how dialogue can and must
be restarted when he spoke off the cuff in San Francisco about
voters who cling to issues because they feel their way of life
threatened by so many aspects of modern change. Indeed, one
can hardly imagine a more perceptive and empathetic analysis
of the opposition, especially in today's political discourse. All
that was lacking was a word or two of outreach ("We need to
reassure these people that their voices are being heard and their
concerns understood".)—which he might well have introduced
in a public forum—to have made these remarks a bell weather of
what political dialogue must include.

Of course, there is always a place for crafting one's remarks,
and much of what George Lakoff has to say can and must be
taken to heart. It would not, for instance, take a Lakoff to
identify the weakness in using Woody Allen's "shark" remark
as more than an arch simile for the progressive view of politics. But progressives must be careful not to respond to the often extreme diatribe coming from the opposition by using the
same, or even remotely similar tactics. I was troubled, in this

respect, by another of Lakoff's commentaries—"Progressives Lack a Limbaugh-Like Voice"[9]—in which he said that while the forces of the conservative right have a Rush Limbaugh who can rally the troops, progressives do not: Democrats need to "communicate" more. While the sentiment is sound, the association is weak, even dangerous. To evoke—at length—one of the most regressive voices in American democracy today as an argument for progressives doing a better job of communicating is to slip much too closely to the suggestion that we need a Limbaugh. But nothing could be further from the truth.

Limbaugh and his ilk are entitled to their political views: I reside in a country which prohibits the publication of *Mein Kampf*, and I think that is a serious violation of democratic values. But in a democratic society, opposition to views one disagrees with must take place in an atmosphere of dialogue—what Obama calls, in his second book, " a conversation . . . in which all citizens are required to engage" if the perils of concentration of power are to be avoided. That conversation must be judicious, reflective, open and inclusive, and while it will inevitably—and necessarily—be full of feeling at times, the true aims of those who speak will be identifiable in the feelings they evoke as they do. Progressive politics in America does not need a Rush Limbaugh—or anyone like him—to rally its forces because, by definition, *that kind of rallying point deals in the manipulation of raw emotions, shorthand analysis and simplistic solutions.*

We don't need a Limbaugh. We need to trust the American people to distinguish between the hysterical and the thoughtful, the manipulative and the pursuasive. We need to speak in a language that promotes dialogue—even when the other side may not be ready to engage us. We need to ground ourselves in

9   http://www.truthout.org/042609Y

a tone—*gravitas*—which recognizes both the gravity of the tasks before us, the responsibility that goes with facing those tasks, and the conviction that we are capable of responding to them. In short, we need *vision*.

V

The quality of the feelings a political perspective evokes is central to its vision for those it purports to serve. Resentment, fear, hunger for retribution, frustration at the complexities of modern life: these are among the deeper feelings upon which the right wing core of the Republican Party has played since the beginning of the so-called Reagan Revolution—though one could argue that validation of those feelings in post-war American politics really began with Spiro Agnew. These feelings are also the core elements of the more hysterical attitudes which, normally consigned to the fringe of any political discourse, have—troublingly—entered the mainstream of American political discourse via the media masters of resentful politics, the Pat Buchanans, the Jerry Falwells and the Limbaughs—and now the Tea Party. And it does not take a master of political rhetoric to see that, beneath the sometimes thin surface of their "political" punditry, these figures harbor a deep antagonism of precisely the kind Sarah Palin displayed with her hockey mom/pitbull characterization. The distance between the vengeful view of political retribution—say, towards the "liberal media elite"—implied in the emotions these figures evoke and the ghastly comments of anti-abortionists who saw the murder of George Tiller as God's retribution can be measured in micrometers.

One of the reasons this manipulation is so effective is precisely that it allows emotions full expression in a time when many people are suffering from emotional overload. But there is a world of difference between the kind of expression of emotion which leads us to deeper reflection and the venting which becomes itself an emotional opiate, blocking any real understanding of the problems we face. In the past, for better and for worse, the American Dream served as a kind of transducer for emotions of all kinds, allowing immigrants from a wide range of backgrounds to share means and ends—all with the hope of a better future. But the American Dream is a relic of the past. The basis upon which the "better life" of material well-being could be established has long been in place, and it has been extended to all but a few. The importance of that last qualification is not trivial, as we shall see. But the simple truth is that the life to which generations of immigrants aspired has been achieved. The American Dream can no longer serve as an emotional cathexis any more than the idea of the Frontier can.

Moreover, to identify something that would channel the emotions of Americans and Americans alone would be to take a step backward. America can no longer hope—nor should it want—to "lead the world" in the way that it did during the relatively short period period of its ascendancy in the 20th century. Other countries have better standards of living, others offer greater security to those who live under their social umbrellas, and many others now demonstrate the drive and the passion to succeed that brought America to the privileged place it once occupied.

If progressive political thinking is to provide a real alternative to the often very dark forces that have again begun to assemble on the horizon of the social landscape, not only in America, but in the global reality of which America is only a part, then that alternative will have to provide a more ecumenical view than that offered by the American Dream. Moreover it will also have to offer a view that can carry the weight of the emotions now in play: the frustrations felt by those who fear change; the anticipations of those who see the world operating at closer and closer quarters; and the aspirations of millions who would give anything to share the wealth that is presently enjoyed by so few. I can think of only two words which can embody all those things.

One of them is "vision". For vision implies something elevated, something to aspire to, something that guides us in a search for higher goods and higher truths, something that allows us all, as the American Dream once did for Americans, to become more than we now are. But vision is a tricky thing: it can be put in the service of movements which intimate higher values only to prove themselves tools of lesser gods, as Napoleon, Lenin, Hitler, Mussolini, and Mao—among so many others—have demonstrated. Which is why we need a second word: democratic. The word speaks for itself. It evokes everything progressive thinking stands for: the people, their right to determine their own lives, and their dependence on one another if the world they choose to build is to survive.

If progressive political thinking is to gain the attention and galvanize the emotions of those who confront both an endless materialistic wasteland and the inevitable—and perhaps even rapid—decline that will set in if we remain aimless, it must offer something that can avoid the hyperbole of so many contemporary political messages, the tepid cliches of others *and* the demagoguery which is so rapidly taking over the landscape of political discourse. And it must be based on trust in a people's ability to recognize a perceptive argument, recognition of the vital place of dialogue in political discourse, and a sense of the gravity of the tasks we face. I propose that we call that something the Democratic Vision.

Cognomens like these, of course, run the risk of being seen as trite, hollow, self-important, or just plain silly. (Who, of those of us who lived in those times, can forget the pathetic WIN—"Whip Inflation Now"—buttons of Gerald Ford?) But they need not be: the New Deal meant something in its time and still does three-quarters of a century later; the New Frontier, though it evoked as much a sentiment as it did an action plan, captured a feeling that had real, if tragically short-lived, historical import; and slogans like "We Shall Overcome", "Eyes on the Prize" and "I Have a Dream" carry with them all the force of a Negro spiritual and a social crusade. The real test of a name lies in how well it captures the aspirations it tries to coalesce.

The word "vision" has the strength of elevating our discussions without making them so ephemeral as to be bromides. True, anyone can have a vision, and the vision can be as mundane or as debased as it can elevated. But perhaps the real importance of the word emerged, in an inverted form, when then-Vice President George H. W. Bush made his infamous "Oh, the vision thing", remark in response to suggestions that he look at the larger picture rather than the day-to-day strategy of campaigning for the nation's highest office. The fact that the remark has virtually entered the language as an epithet for a politician's failure to offer a more elevated view of how the world should be indicates that people still expect leadership that offers an elevated perspective. For all the appeal of a folksy, "down home" George W. Bush, or the mock-populism of Sarah Palin, people expect something that allows them to aspire, to hope. Demagogues in populist clothing from Fr. Coughlin to Sarah Palin may make short-term inroads into the public mind, but it takes a "Gettysburg Address" or a phrase like FDR's "fear itself" or JFK's "ask not", to evoke truly visionary notions of what a people can aspire to be.

More demanding, and yet more self-evident in its import, is the word "Democratic".

Perhaps no one has more succinctly distilled the essence of democracy than Lincoln did when he called it "government of the people, by the people and for the people". Democracy guarantees that a people—and *all* the people who lay claim to membership in it—will decide for themselves how they are to be governed. Period. While notions of liberty, equality, franternity, the pursuit of happiness and a whole host of others may be subject to discussion and interpretation, the word "democracy" is fairly straightforward. What progressives must confront head-on is not the nature of democracy, but the question of its validity: if we give a people the right to choose the ways and means with which they are governed, will they choose wisely? After all, the American people chose Richard Nixon, Ronald Reagan and George W. Bush—each for two terms, when one would have hoped the first term might have given them pause for thought. There is, of course, a complex corollary to each of the six elections mentioned in that last sentence: the electorate chose each of the successful candidates over one or two other candidates, not from a broad pool of "the best and the brightest" available candidates, and each of those choices took place in the context of an environment—rampant social unrest in Nixon's case, stagflation and "malaise" in Reagan's, and (leaving aside the question of whether the electorate actually chose George W. Bush in 2000) the September 11th attacks in 2004—which contributed powerfully to the election's outcome.

Which brings us back to Maslow. Maslow says that, given satisfaction of the basic needs they require, most people will opt for growth—for things that solidify their level of satisfaction *and* allow them to expand outwardly and upwardly. In other words, given the opportunity to choose reflectively, people will choose wisely. There is no reason to think that democratic choices will take place any differently.

Given a stable and secure foundation, people in a democracy can be expected to choose wisely. *That* must be the *ne plus ultra* of any progressive credo, and it must be believed and practiced by those who subscribe to it. This underlines the need for trust in the people who participate in a democracy, but it also reveals what a responsible, enlightened progressive agenda must do in the face of environmental factors which may affect peoples' choices, from economic upheaval to perceived external threat: *a progressive political perspective must continue to stand for the truth, firmly—and when necessary, loudly—in whatever social or political context it faces.* In other words, in the midst of environmental factors which may have an undue impact on peoples' perception of what is genuinely in their best interest, progressives need to serve as a beacon, not only for helping people to identify their real best interest, but to *elevate* the discussion that ensues.

The aftermath of the September 11th attacks is a prime example.

In the months following attacks which were arguably more traumatic, and perhaps more a turning point in American history, than Pearl Harbor, it was common to speak of them as signifying the "loss of American innocence". Leaving aside all the parsing of assumptions that could be done of that phrase, the tragedy of the aftermath was that there was no attempt to see the attacks as a coming of age. For too long, Americans had lived in a gauze-like cocoon detached from what was really taking place in the world of the late twentieth century. The OJ Simpson trial got vastly more attention than famine in Sudan;

Monica Lewinsky more than the Yangtze River floods. The 9/11 attacks were a wake-up call, not for America to "defend" itself, but for the most powerful country on earth to begin to see that the upheaval going on among the least powerful was leading to sociopathic desperation. The clarion call of America's response to the attacks was—mindlessly, even from the most fundamental of foreign policy perspectives—to declare "war" on an enemy which had no status as a nation. While some defensive measure had to be taken—and the invasion of Afghanistan, had it been prudently and exclusively pursued, was probably one of them—the real challenge for America at that point was to invoke a vision that would reach out to those on the edge of desperation and give them hope, to say "we stand with you, we hear you". That message need not have precluded moral outrage, determination to bring the sociopaths to justice, or even a warning that future attacks would not be tolerated. But a truly reflective and judicious—and democratic—vision would have recognized that it was in America's – and the developed world's – best interests to ally themselves with those whose plight made them vulnerable to seeing the sociopaths as heros.

The opportunity to make outreach a major part of the West's response to 9/11 was effectively lost even before the attacks took place, when George W. Bush was awarded the Presidency by the Supreme Court—though one wonders how much more judicious a response would have come from a Gore administration. But the fact that almost no one on the Left made anything but the most remote gestures in this direction after the attacks is deeply troubling.[10] Progressives got on the "war" bandwagon,

10 Telllingly, Senator Patty Murray (D-Washington) made just such a speech and her subsequent Republican opponent used sound bites from it in his campaign against her. She won that campaign.

and few stopped before the wagon reached Bagdhad 18 months later. At a time when progressives could have—admittedly, at considerable political risk—staked out ground that would endure the tumult and the shouting of the subsequent seven years, the opportunity was not lost: it was never even recognized. And today, a decade after the attacks, little has been said or done that would point Americans towards an understanding of what terrorism really represents, let alone to make outreach a part of its response to the attacks.[11]

A Democratic Vision would have provided that understanding, but only if it extended itself beyond the confines of the United States, the EU, Western-style industrial democracies and even developed countries in general. A Democratic Vision will be nothing if it is not universal. It must allow the progressive political perspective to make one of its cornerstones the fact that we live in an age which demands the democratic tradition—"of the people, by the people and for the people"—be extended to *all*.

This will be no easy task. One must immediately ask how "the people", let alone their best interests, are to be identified in North Korea, Iran, China, or the Occupied Territories. But embracing a Democratic Vision does not provide progressives with a cure-all or a methodological skeleton key that will unlock solutions to every problem. What it does offer is a beacon of reflection and judiciousness that can be cast on every issue, and a touchstone that can be invoked in the midst of dialogue about those issues. There will always be difficult questions to be asked:

---

11 It should also be said that progressives have failed to drive home another vital message about the September 11 attacks: terrorists, by definition, try to so unbalance an outsized opponent that it falls of its own weight and ineptitude; in its repeated and flagrant violation of democratic values in response to the attacks, the Bush administration very nearly handed them a substantive, as well as a moral victory.

does this allocation of funds serve the purpose at hand? will resolving this border dispute with a concession of land bring the conflict to a close? will this distribution of representation balance out the interests of diverse populations? But one can only expect democratic traditions to do their work in an environment in which a Democratic Vision is held uppermost in the minds of those at the table—or in the voting booth. And progressives must (and one can hope that, one day, conservatives might) accept the responsibility of abandoning hyperbole and "speaking truth to the people", if you will, whatever the short-term political costs.

This may seem a naïve, idealistic, almost quixotic path to take in an era in which politcal strategy and maneuver have become the object of billions of dollars of research, policy wonking and spin. But it is not.

Three decades ago, in a period when deep inertia threatened to set in among those who had tried to oppose the totalitarian policies of the Brezhnev era in then-Eastern Europe, Vaclav Havel wrote an essay that re-energized dissidents with a simple declaration, contained in the essay's title, that despite all appearances to the contrary the powerless in the Warsaw Pact countries were actually empowered by the mileu which the "post-totalitarian" system, as he called it, had created.[12] In that system, he argued, a verneer of normalcy had been spread across a life of deep spiritual poverty: in return for stability and mild (by Western standards) creature comforts, the rank and file in Czechoslovakia, Poland, Hungary and their "socialist brother" states had agreed to act as though particiation in non-election elections, deference to Party policy and, above all, the

---

12 "The Power of the Powerless", in *Open Letters: Selected Writings, 1965– 1990* (New York: Knopf, 1991).

self-censorship of one's political opinions, were normal. In that unremittingly grey mileu, Havel said, to "live in truth" was to act as a beacon of laser-like intensity, to say that the emperor had no clothes was to deliver a thunderclap which could not be silenced by Soviet-style Marxist ideology, nuclear arms or the secret police. Time proved Havel right: the revolutions of 1989 might never have caught fire as they did had there not been the many beacons of light that punctuated the 40-year darkness and, by the contrast they established, had they not kept –as one might say happened for a time in Romania—people from being blinded by the dazzling light of the new day that dawned.

Our times and our mileu are not so dark as those experienced under forty years of Soviet domination in the old Warsaw Pact countries, but the two are not without their similarities. One of the remarkable things about Havel's essay is how central what he calls "the consumer value system" is to his argument. With shops, to a greater or lesser degree, full, employment guaranteed and cultural modes such as non-threatening music, drama and film supported, sometimes lavishly, by the state, the common people could go about their lives with a semblance of reality, ignoring the socialist slogans in the shop windows, the non-choice elections and the impossibility of travel outside the Soviet bloc. A life of modest consumption allowed them to ape normalcy, dismissing their total lack of political freedom with a helpless shrug: "What can we do? We are so powerless, and 'they' are so powerful".

How much more is our own mileu caught up in, not modest, but extravagant, even garish consumption? And how much more likely is it that we in the Western democracies, while we may still have some element of influence over political realities, will give our own shrug of powerlessness and return to our televisions, internet sites and the countless toys that modern industrial life makes available to us? And particularly in America, though with alarmingly increasing frequency in other Western industrialized societies, how much is the obsession with accumulating "toys" an opiate that we use to distract ourselves from the magnitude of the political realities we face, not to mention the deepening spiritual poverty we experience?

This powerlessness and the frustration it creates underpin phenomenae like Sarah Palin, Rush Limbaugh and the Tea Party movement. These purveyors of mindlessly simple solutions to monumentally complex problems draw on precisely the awareness that all is not well which Havel said dissidents must keep alive if society were not to fall into an ideologically induced slumber in the Soviet-dominated countries of central Europe. In the industrialized West, we do not face the almost impenetrable darkness imposed by the secret police. But we do face the danger of letting a consumer value system overwhelm our better selves, and we face the added danger of allowing political opportunists and demagogues—some of them clearly supported by those who would perpetuate the stupor of consumption simply to achieve the profit margins they set for themselves—to harness emotions that, for want of an alternative, would lead to a reactionary blight that could set democracy back, not just decades, but centuries.

Progressives represent an alternative to harnessing those emotions. And they owe it to themselves and to those who experience the frustration that is so commonly felt on the left as well as the right, to offer, not simply an alternative to the Palins and the Lumbaughs, but to the frustrating social, political and emotional landscape we all inhabit. We are not so far removed from the reality Havel and his contemporaries faced: there is a crisis; it is a crisis that threatens the very fabric of our world; and our most powerful tool in addressing the many facets of that crisis is to tell the truth, quietly and calmly, in a way that can be recognized and understood by those who see—or simply feel—the effects the crisis is having on our way of life.

What is that crisis? It is, quite simply, the crisis of direction for humankind and the world that Western development has led it into. We have reached a pinnacle in our journey out of the savannahs of Central Africa, one which affords some of us a life of astonishing ease, comfort, security and freedom. But we do not know what to do with that life. Because so many of its positive features rely on humankind's increasing access material wealth, we have allowed ourselves to become obsessively attached to the notion that wealth is everything. Yet we sense that it is not, that it does not bring with it the deeper satisfaction that we all want: we find ourselves, as Stringfellow Barr put it over half a century ago, "waiting for something that never arrived". Moreover, we know subliminally that the bulk of the planet's population benefits little, if at all, from the wealth we do enjoy, and that there is something irresponsible, even morally culpable, about that fact if we do nothing to insure that others have access to what we enjoy.

Only a true Democratic Vision can solve the conundrum of malaise in the face of wealth that Western democracies increasingly experience. Some of that vision must be applied in our own spheres, where, as so many have shown, a lack of ease, comfort, security and freedom plagues even those within societies of affluence and conspicuous consumption. But in the world of the 21st century and beyond, a progressive political perspective cannot stop there. It must expand its horizons, not simply rhetorically but existentially, to shine the beacon of real democratic values—real progressive truth-telling—on the problems which exist among the two-thirds of humankind who do not, cannot enjoy the luxury of directionlessness. To do so will be to establish direction for the directionless, and power for the powerless, in ways only the truth can.

VI

It would be easy—and fundamentally dishonest—to end this discussion on a ringing note of profound commitment to democratic values for all. But a real Democratic Vision can only emerge in an atmosphere of dialogue. Moroever, as has been said several times, a vision based on such democratic values is not a sword that will slice through every Gordian knot we face. Discussion, some of it troublingly complex, will be required on a whole range of problems if we are even to begin to map out the landscape on which we find ourselves, let alone the paths we must take. So let's take a full frontal look at some of those problems and how an enlightened Democratic Vision might deal with them. (Let me be clear: this is not a list of policies or a suggestion about a "one right way" to address a given political issue. Each is an illustration of the ways in which an enlightened progressive perspective can be brought to bear on issues of importance with force and, provided the effort is consistent and determined, success. Other ways may and probably do exist. One of the discussions that must take place is how to prioritize various approaches so as to keep from dissipating their impact with the scatter-shot style that has been so prevalent on the left and so taken advantage of by the right.)

The first problem, while not one of the kind we normally think of in policy terms, is nonetheless a real and very compelling one which we have already mentioned: the degree to which demagoguery and hysteria have begun to cast a shadow over the political landscape, not only in America, but in other industrial democracies as well. We discussed this problem above, but let's isolate it and address it once more: whether the issue is immigration, economic policy, the environment, social welfare or the role of government in daily life, demagogues—like the Lumbaughs and Palins, the LePens, the British Nationalists and the Tea Party—have begun to set the agenda by virtue of the volume of their attacks and the resentments those attacks play on.

The only reponse to this increasingly dangerous phenomenon (and we must see it as a unified phenomenon, not as a set of distinct, or only loosely related developments) is a progressive discourse that combines *gravitas* and truth-telling to create the basis for real discussion and dialogue. Barack Obama's "round-table" with members of Congress on the health care reform bill had elements of this. It was a reasonable, collegial and very democratic attempt to bring people together for discussion in an atmosphere of dialogue. Of course, it did not pan out that way as the day went on: Republican grand-standing assured that real discussion would not take place. But if there was something missing, it was a real sense of *gravitas* on the part of the Democrats. Rarely (the exception of Dick Durbin comes to mind) did one *feel* the great urgency of the issue at hand, the great tragedy of American backwardness on the issue of health care when compared with the rest of the Western democracies. When Congressman Paul Ryan remarked, melodramatically, that under the British health care system, his mother could not have obtained a drug she badly needed, no one scolded him for his crass dissembling: "Of course she could obtain the drug, John", someone should have said, "she simply would have had to pay for it herself. And one lapse in an overwhelmingly successful system is not a justification for backing away from national health care, it's an object lesson on how to do it even better". While a remark like that might seem to be inflammatory, it is not; delivered judiciously and with a sober tone of calm conviction, it would be seen for what it is: honesty and gravity appropriate to the setting, the problem—and to the prevarication that is being presented as proof. No one said dialogue and discussion had to be courtly.

But what of some of the more identifiable policy issues of the day that divide societies—abortion, for instance?

Progressives must begin with one painful truth: abortion is not a pretty thing. Whether you defend the right of a woman to make decisions about her body in consultation with a doctor of her choice—as I do—or whether you believe that abortion is murder, the simple fact is that, in a moral order that puts human life at the top of its pyramid of priorities, the termination of even a potential life is something that most of us would prefer not to do. That reality need not be lingered upon, but neither can it be denied, and progressives would be lying to soft-pedal it. But without becoming lost in an infinite parsing of the question about whether or not an empryo is a human being (Augustine and Aquinas, though they both opposed abortion, said that it was not), we can come at the problem of abortion by way of an approach that emphasizes our sympathy with the conservative attitude.

Abortion, we can say, is a less than desirable procedure, but in many cases it is also a "preventable" procedure. The available prevention is widely available birth control and appropriate sex education of the kind is so frequently opposed by conservative religious groups. Statistics show that abortions are overwhelmingly sought by unmarried women, particularly those under the age of 25, and particularly those from impoverished or minority backgrounds. In other words, abortion is—whether we like it or not—often a method of birth control after the fact of conception. Religious groups and right wing demagogues whip these facts up into a froth of self-righteous indignation, moral approbation, and not a little racism: "unwed mothers", "welfare queens", etc., etc. are the "real" problem. The real problem is lack of education—real education, in which sexually active women *and* men learn to integrate birth control into their normal practices—and lack of access.

A serious, thoughtful message like this sends out a number of important signals. It acknowledges a conservative's right to believe in the sanctity of life, but it does so in a way that encourages him or her to do what can be done to limit the circumstances in which abortion may be seen as an option. While that will not resolve the debate between those who feel an embryo or fetus has rights and those who disagree, it does extend some respect to those who take the most conservative position. They may not accept or even acknowledge that gesture, but they themselves are not the only target group: the overwhelming majority of Americans (this is largely an American issue, though not entirely) accept that there are cases in which abortion should be allowed; that base will be strengthened, and perhaps expanded considerably, by a progressive stance that respects the minority view but puts common sense first.

Gun control is another issue which, while almost uniquely American, would benefit from some simple, and again respectful, untying of the emotional knots which have been used by the right to entangle the issue. In congressional hearings not long ago, a woman whose mother and father had been killed by a man firing randomly in a coffee shop spoke tearfully of what might have happened had laws permitted him to carry his firearm with him wherever he went.[13] The implication was, of course, that the father could have used his weapon to defend himself, his wife, and the other patrons of the coffee shop. None of the members of the committee was able to respond to the woman or her logic, even though a powerful—and respectful—response was available. Any member of the committee could have expressed deep sympathy for the woman's loss, but then asked her what good it would have done the other victims in the coffee shop if her father had been allowed to carry his gun but had left before the shooter entered. Her only reply would have had to be that, without legal restrictions on carrying weapons, "hopefully someone else would have been carrying a gun". At which point the questioner could have pointed out that the woman's solution—looser controls on carrying firearms—would ensure public safety *only if everyone, or at least the large majority of citizens, were carrying weapons*. In other words, extending her logic out to protect everyone in public places would require a return to the old West.

Here again, the object of unravelling the emotional logic of a moving testimony is not to win an argument, or even to change the minds of those who believe that "when guns are outlawed, only outlaws will have guns". The point is first to show appreciation and respect for those who, wrongly, think that

---

13 A similar sentiment, but expressed in an unbelievably callow manner, came from a candidate for Congress from Virginia in the 2010 election when he said that the Virginia Tech massacre could have been averted if one of the students in one of the classrooms had been "packin' heat". That candidate lost the campaign. But a short two years later, the tragic shooting of Gabrielle Giffords and 19 others was met with some voices insisting greater freedom to carry firearms would have prevented the shooting.

widespread gun ownership is a solution, or would have been a solution, to perceived or actual danger. Secondly, the aim must be to unmask the sometimes gaping flaws in emotional logic that so frequently get overlooked. An honest and understanding recognition of the temptation to believe that a simplistic solution offers a real answer, followed up by a sober assessment of what costs are often hidden beneath the surface of simplistic thinking, may not change minds; but it will reduce the power of an emotional argument and stand as an illustration of the way emotional issues must be addressed.

While both abortion and gun control are issues most apparent in American political discourse, others are more common to all industrial democracies and not the least of those is the question of immigration. I use the term "immigration", not "illegal immigration", because to focus on the "illegal" aspect of immigration is to miss the point. While the breaking of the law implied in the entry of undocumented workers into a country may be a hook upon which many hang their discontent, that is rarely the source of their real concern. One need only listen to, or read, the personal accounts of, for instance, the perception that "the reason our emergency rooms are so full and you can't see a doctor is because of all *those* people" (a remark I have heard from someone living in Texas and someone else living in Toronto) to know that, at the very least, the concern in many industrial democracies is that their societies are being overrun by "foreigners".

Whether one speaks of France, the UK, Italy, the Netherlands, the US, Canada—or indeed, of many developing countries: large numbers of Somalis and Ethiopians, for instance, currently make their way into Yemen illegally—there can be no doubt that we are talking about a single phenomenon of global and historical proportions. In raw numbers, and partly because of globalization in all its forms, we are witnessing the largest population migrations the planet has ever seen. No country is immune, no border impenetrable, and no policy change or action agenda—wall, "fence", electronic grid, or whatever—can change the situation. We may as well try to build a barrier to the migrations of birds or the movement of the tides. The question is not how to stop it, but how to cope with it.

In this respect, Americans should be far out in front of the pack for the simple and historically inescapable reason that, whatever holes may exist in American mythologies, America is and always has been a nation of immigrants. What many Americans fail to realize is that, in defiance of the myth perpetuated by the "give me your tired, your homeless, etc". rhetoric on the Statue of Liberty, nativisim—the resistance to immigration—has always been a strong force in American history. Opposition to "illegal immigration" in the US today is simply a new nativism, amplified by the fact that a huge portion of the incoming migrants come from Spanish speaking countries—and thereby elicit the hostility of those who resist the multi-cultural values inherent in things like bilingual education. Attitudes in EU countries are not much different.

But one thing that unites the EU, Canada, the US and many other industrial democracies—as well as non-industrial, non-democracies in many parts of the world—is the fact that *the migrants who come into these countries are, by and large, needed by the economies of the countries to which they migrate.* The notion that Mexicans are taking away jobs from Americans, Arabs from the French, Turks from the Germans and the Dutch is simply not true—a fact historically underscored by the *bracero* programs of the US, the *gasterbeiter* program in Germany and *gastarbeider* programs in the Netherlands and Belgium, which served to prime the pump of migrant labor flow throughout the 20th century. Ironically (though not suprisingly, given its roots in a border state), the last Bush administration came closest to uttering the unuttrable: were it possible to eliminate all undocumented workers from the US (or German, Dutch, Italian, etc.) economy in a day, the economy would go into free fall the next. But no one wants to admit this openly out of fear of the public uproar it would produce.

In some cases there can be a wisdom to moving gradually towards a full statement of the truth, and this is one. Most Americans are not ready to hear that their economy would teeter on the brink of collapse if it lost an asset which many, if not most, see as a liability. But herein lies a golden opportunity to educate the public, gradually but firmly, and to invert the polarities which generally put the business world in the conservative camp. A comprehensive rethink of immigration policy is necessary, but a comprehensive policing operation—which is what most Americans probably think of when they hear about "the immigration problem"—is not the answer. Progressives must take the lead in explaining the truth about immigration to the American public, and in marshalling support for an honest reappraisal from the millions of small businesses and individuals who rely on cheap labor from other countries to stay afloat. Progressives in other countries must do the same.

It is only from a firm base of understanding our reliance on undocumented workers that any effective reappraisal of immigration can be made. Proposed solutions may vary from "amnesty" programs to renewed guest worker programs, and no doubt blends suited to a given country of the many options that exist will be the best way to proceed. But there is another element of public policy which must be brought to bear on the discussion about immigration, and it is one which must become the centerpost of progressive thought in every country, bar none. It involves the equal sharing of opportunities and resources.

Seen from almost any angle, the goal of equitable sharing of resources must be the foundation of any consolidated progressive effort to influence, not only domestic politics in a given country, but to address the larger, global issues which increasingly involve virtually every country, every constituency and every individual voter. If progressives make a Democratic Vision the cornerstone of their agenda and recognize the stepwise fashion in which, as Maslow says—and as the path of Western countries through industrialization into affluence demonstrates—humankind moves towards, not merely the enjoyment of creature comforts, but habits of mind which confront social problems with an eye for solutions based in everything from morality to creativity, then the real challenge facing the twenty-first century is how to use the tools gained and the lessons learned from the last two centuries to lift the entire human population to a level of material safety and security—though not necessarily excessive consumption—on a par with industrialized democracies.

There is a fly in the ointment of that approach, to be sure. For one faces, not simply the task of convincing electorates in different countries and cultures that their preoccupations must shift from the acquisition of creature comforts to sharing their success with others still standing in line for entrance into the world of affluence that has been created, but the additional task of sufficiently ensuring the security and stability of those with a modicum of affluence that they will be able to even listen to the argument that others should be brought into the world they occupy. For Maslow's model works both ways: take away security and stability, and less magnanimous impulses take over—tragically so when the stars are aligned to permit it, as was the case in Germany after World War I. So one of the pieces that must be put into place if progressives are to help turn the regional successes of the past into a program for global success in the future is a guarantee of stability and security for those who must be convinced to turn their gaze outward. Paradoxically, this places progressives in the position of having to take what might be called a conservative economic stance.

Typically, the one place in which political conservatives have tended to be liberal is in their attitude towards free enterprise: free flow of goods and capital, lack of encumbering governmental regulations, reward for those who take the initiative and excel—these are all things that political conservatives tend to support, almost religiously, in the marketplace. Let's leave aside for the moment that much of this is cant which ignores the extent to which business—most especially at the corporate level—relies on everything from government contracts to government bailouts to do what it does. The more profit there is, the conservaties tell us, the more "prosperous" we are, and the invisible hand of the marketplace should be the only determiner of the growth which provides those profits. But the free enterprisers have never addressed the fact that, even assuming their model to be accurate, opportunists and hypocrites—not to mention voracious predators—can manipulate the system, generate profit, and not only undermine the system but put it and all those in it at risk. The near-cataclysmic breakdown of the world financial system in 2008 was only the most recent example of this uncomfortable truth. Moreover, the success of demagoguery in the 2010 elections underlines the ways in which, when their security and stability are at risk, voters will respond, sometimes with great enthusiasm, to simplistic solutions, even when the essence of those solutions goes against their best interests.

The financial crisis of 2008 was nothing if not an object lesson in the fact that Western economies have been gripped by a mania that ignores the fundamental welfare of the societies which economies purport to act on behalf of. Moreover, that mania has as its only justification the expansion of material wealth which, as we have seen, is already well into the range of nonessential comforts and which provides little of the satisfaction the American Dream once seemed to hold out to those who embraced it. In other words, the economic security and stability on which we all rely, not merely for creature comforts, but as a guarantee that anxiety and fear do not so overwhelm us that we lose our democratic balance, has been—and no doubt is still being—put at risk in the name of material gain that is both concentrated at the top of the economic pyramid and, even when it reaches the middle strata of society, contributes little if anything to our deeper sense of satisfaction with our lives.

Progressives have spoken, sometimes eloquently, not only about the unequal income distribution in Western democracies, but about the deep injustice that unequal distribution represents. Especially in the United States, but also in the UK, that argument has come up against a deep strain of belief in self-help, self-reliance, "earning your own way", and all the other clichés that underlie the attitudes Tonnies and Weber long ago traced to religious Puritanism. In the face of that strain, progressives have been stymied by their inability to come up with any rationale for challenging the status quo other than those based on benevolence and fraternal feelings of empathy for the less-well-off—attitudes and efforts the conservatives commonly label "charity", or "welfare". While EU countries provide a much wider and more inclusive safety net than the United States—and France, which is traditionally more concerned with "solidarity" than "self-help", does so better than most—even in these countries the accumulation of wealth at the top has proceeded apace, and the risks that have been taken to assure profits that allow that accumulation have grown proportionately. The crises in Greece, Ireland and Portugal attest to the fact that so-called "free market" principles run the catastrophic risk of putting an economy in free fall.

If progressives are to respond effectively to the "self-help" ethic which has been spreading with the Anglo-Americanization of economic attitudes and business practices throughout the industrialized world, they need to come at the problem from an angle which will not violate, or at least come directly into conflict with, that ethic. And such an angle exists.

Progressives must—again, soberly, firmly and unremittingly—insist that the stability of the economic system be put before the profit motive. While it is absolutely true that circumstances—from historical to environmental—have contributed powerfully to the success of what the Brandt Commission once called "The North", it also remains true that the interwoven realities of history, access to resources and hard work have produced an affluent population that has a right to expect security and stability—though, as we'll see in a moment, that right exists only if those who claim it are willing to share it. Put simply, *the right to security and stability must take precedence over considerations of free enterprise.*

Economic activity in the name of survival is a freedom: no one should impede our ability to ensure our basic needs. But economic activity in an advanced industrial society—or in any society in which the web of interdependence guarantees that the economic activity of one will impact significantly the lives of others—involves *license*: the sanction of that activity by those upon whom it has a significant impact. In fact, in today's advanced industrial societies, economic activity of the kind engaged in by large corporations, multinational groups and financial entities should be seen as a *public trust*. The profit motive alone does not guarantee that corporations will serve the public interest. On the contrary, as the economic history of the twentieth century has shown us time and time again, a preoccupation with the profit motive at the expense of larger question of public welfare may blind actors in the economic sector to the interests of the very (and usually very limited) shareholders they purport to serve.

Progressives must put this message at the forefront of their stance on economic issues: businesses must be held accountable for their impact on the public welfare—and not just in times of crisis, as has all too often been the case. Moreover, the old assumptions surrounding economic growth—most especially the assumption that bigger or more is better—can no longer be allowed to hold exclusive sway over our economic outlook. Long-term economic stability—stability which factors in, not only such things as creation of jobs, but also the risks of instability, including environmental degradation or catastrophe—and a judicious de-emphasis of the need for expanding non-essential creature comforts must take center stage in the progressive prospectus, and those features must be explained in direct and honest terms.

This would be a call for a sea-change in Western economic philosophy—or perhaps more accurately, a dramatic change of course for the body politic, social and economic. Right now, we run the risk of running aground on reefs of risk-taking and shoals of mindless, unsatisfying materialism. Ships of the size of Western capitalism do not change course easily or quickly, and such a change can only be seen as a long-term affair. But it would be foolish to think that a change of direction could be based merely on avoidance of dangers which it may take one or two generations to acknowledge as real. A new direction and a new set of goals must be identified if people in affluent societies are to reshape their entire view of what they are about; but such a direction is part and parcel—in fact at the heart of—anything that deserves the name Democratic Vision.

The late Viktor Frankl once commented on the irony of the existence of a "crisis of meaning" in the West when there were so many profoundly meaningful issues facing the world.[14] Nothing much has changed in the three decades since Frankl made his remarks, except perhaps the fact that the world has grown progressively smaller even as the number of issues requiring urgent attention has grown larger. Simple, even common-sensical appeals to magnanimity and Christian charity have their impact on some when we begin to speak about the hunger, disease, poverty and war that plague much of the world's population, but the real impact of such appeals on problems of the magnitude we face is negligible. Moreover, there is always lurking in the background the sometimes overt, sometimes latent conviction that charity is a stop-gap measure and that the poor, at home and abroad, must learn to "pull themselves up by their bootstraps", that too much help is an opiate that will make them dependent rather than self-sufficient.

Even *gravitas* is not enough in this situation. Repeated reminders, like that of The Hunger Project, that 24 people die of hunger in the world *every minute*, 18 of them children, do little more than create insensibility, even among those who find the figures appalling. However, most appeals to members of affluent societies about these problems rely, understandably, on an implicit assumption of the inequality that exists between the affluent and the poor: the affluent are encouraged to help in an appeal to charity that is as old as human history. But in a democratic society, few people want to be benefactors, particularly as

14 "The Meaning Crisis in the First World and Hunger in the Third World", *International Forum for Logotherapy* 7, no, 1.

a full-time occupation; assuming that stance puts us in a superior position that we, understandably, find uncomfortable. But much the opposite seems to be true when members of an affluent community are dealing with disasters which have struck them.

Stories of communities pulling together in the face of floods, fires, earthquakes and other disasters are almost part of the daily news cycle in a globalized world. People who throw open their homes to those who have lost theirs, workers who leave their jobs when a call goes out for disaster relief assistance, are a staple of news stories about natural—and unnatural—disasters. But these kinds of assistance usually assume an underlying *equality*, even if only by virtue of the fact that those in need of assistance are somehow seen as members of the same community as those providing it. Mutuality often supercedes things like economic and social difference; tragedy, as has been known for centuries, has the power to bring us together in fellowship. Moreover, especially in America I have been struck by the way in which natural disasters can at times create almost a kind of euphoria once the community has been brought together in response: neighbors in a stricken neighborhood can be heard to declare that the disaster was "the best thing that ever happened to them" because it brought them out of the shells of their individual lives and allowed them to establish close, meaningful relationships with neighbors they had hardly known.

It is this last phenomenon which holds the key to undoing the ironic impasse to which Frankl was referring. Given the opportunity to deal caringly with those around them—forced to do so, perhaps, by such things as disasters—people not only respond, but in doing so reap a harvest of deeper satisfaction than their workaday lives generally provide. But they do this most readily when they can feel they occupy some common ground with those they are helping. If progressives are to push the agenda of social justice to which they have naturally and rightly laid claim for decades, they must do so with an eye toward creating a sense of common ground between those who suffer from social injustice and those who do not. And there is an American tradition that offers itself as a basis for establishing just that common ground.

One of the more admirable features of the American immigrant experience, something which goes beyond such things as "the pioneer spirit" and "rugged individualism", and one which has received far too little attention when the American success story is retold and analyzed, is the extent to which immigrants to the US worked hard, not for themselves, but for their children and their children's futures. Paeans to the American spirit talk frequently about the "unlimited opportunities" afforded to the industrious and the hardworking, but few give sufficient attention to the pattern, especially prevalent among immigrants after the Civil War, of those who took menial jobs, not with the hope of achieving affluence themselves, but of providing their children with a foundation—most especially with respect to their education—to achieve what their parents could not.

While care for one's children and their futures is a universal, the notion that the parents work to allow their children to live lives that they themselves could not is one especially characteristic of the immigrant experience—and one which, while typically American in the nineteenth and twentieth centuries, has begun to become global in the migration of populations from poorer to richer countries in the post-World War II period. Moreover, a recurrent theme of political discourse in our own time, on both the Right and the Left, has been concern about the future that a society creates for its children with the decisions it makes today. On the Left one hears this theme repeatedly in concerns expressed about environmental degradation;

on the Right, the theme appears in concerns expressed about government spending and national debt. But taken at face value (which, of course, one must always be careful about doing), the motives behind this theme are the same, and quite similar to the American tradition of "giving my children what I couldn't have".

But in today's America, except perhaps among recent immigrants, and among disenfranchised groups who still struggle to achieve the economic status that race and history have denied them, the notion of working for a better future for our children has a hollow ring, when it exists at all. Where a Spanish refugee from the civil war could come to Brooklyn in the 1930s, take a job as a janitor, and work with real devotion towards providing his children the education and the opportunities he never had, few middle class Americans today would see themselves in the same light. With affluence established as the norm, they may be hard pressed to muster the deep sense of mission and the satisfaction that comes from providing their children with a better life than they had, since "better" can largely only be defined in terms of creature comforts. But that need not be the case, in America or elsewhere.

The emerging concerns about the world we will leave our children and grandchildren are a good sign. While they may sometimes amount to little more than cant, at their best they represent an integration of a new notion into the body politic of Western democracies[15]: the recognition that our actions can no longer be guided by some simple, and probably naïve notion of "progress", that our policies and practices must be guided by a sense of what outcomes they are *really* likely to produce. And in the face of the question of whether or not we are

15 And one woefully absent, at least thus far, in growing economies such as China's.

facing an era of decline or the possibility of a transformative moment, perhaps nothing provides a more reliable basis for action than acknowledging the extent to which what we do we do, not simply for ourselves, but for our children and all those who come after us.

For the question of what we leave to our successors has both immediate and remote implications. Because his father died when he was ten years old, my father grew up in a working class, single parent family.[16] Through the beneficence of an uncle he managed one year of college before entering military service in World War II—an occupation he then held on to for two decades in order to insure the economic welfare and stability of the family he and my mother had begun; she for her part gave up a budding singing career for the same reasons. In precisely the fashion Maslow's model predicts, the economic stability they provided—along with a warm family life and an emphasis on education sustained by my father's perseverance going to night school and getting his bachelor's degree at age 38—gave me the foundation upon which I could make choices that brought me to where I am today. Importantly, I do not concern myself greatly with my children's economic welfare: they enjoy a modest level of affluence and can expect to do so in their few remaining years as my dependents; but they also live in a society in which the social net is strong should anything happen to me, and higher education, by American standards, is virtually without cost. Their financial well-being is as assured as any parent could hope it to be. My concerns for them have more to do with

---

16 Lest the implication be missed, let me point out that, not only was my father fatherless for most of his life, he was effectively raised by his mother and an older sister: as close to a same-sex couple upbringing that was allowed to exist in those days.

the quality of their emotional lives, their appreciation of imagination and insight, and their dedication to social justice and to truth. I count as a blessing the fact that they cannot have all the gadgets and gimmicks their friends have. (I well remember that I got my first hula-hoop weeks after the fad erupted, when the original price of $2.99 had dropped to $.99. Looking back, I count that as a blessing too.)

My debt to my father's working class background is profound; my debt to the sacrifices he and my mother made to have a family is the same. But beyond my personal debt, and the debt my sons owe to my parents, there lies a deeper, more profound influence that our family ties have allowed each of us to benefit from: the sense that what we do for one another we do for everyone.

In my father's second career, in which he served as an employment counselor during Lyndon Johnson's War on Poverty, he became responsible for veteran's employment programs up and down California's Great Valley, later for the entire state. Once, when I spoke to him about the many trips by car he made to Employment Opportunity Centers around the state, I asked him if he had the use of a state car for the trips. "Yeah", he said, "but I just use mine and get reimbursed for the gas. It saves the state wear and tear on one of its cars". In one sense, this could be seen as a form of (some might say perverted) sacrifice. But I think for my father it was something more: making his small— and by the standards of the California super-economy, virtually meaningless—contribution was a gesture of appreciation, even affection, of the kind I recognized he made to my mother, me and my brothers; it was a recognition that we all depend on one another in some way, and that acknowledging that fact through an act of unsolicited benevolence was a source of satisfaction and bonding.

Most parents, while they may not be willing to use their own resources to help defray the costs of a state bureaucracy, would understand doing so for their children. What progressives must learn to do is to provide a basis for extending those feelings out beyond the circle of family and friends to which they normally apply, to explain—unsentimentally but firmly (with *gravitas*, if you will)—that those feelings apply to each and all of us: to individuals, to families (as Margaret Thatcher would have it) and to society at large (as she would not). Progressive thought can build a formidable part of the foundation for its agenda on the ground of family feelings—*real* family values—and on the notion that such feelings bestow, not only a sense of social responsibility and social justice, but of the deep personal satisfaction one feels at devoting oneself to the welfare of all.

This is equally true on the domestic landscape and the international: whether one is speaking of unemployed youths in American inner cities, in the suburbs of French cities or the shanty towns of Soweto, whether one is moved by the plight of underpaid factory workers in Southeast Asia or women getting unequal pay in offices across America, the essence of the relationship between those who hurt and those who help must be built on the common ground of *real* family values, and only a Democratic Vision can provide the basis for putting those values into action. For what is the essence of that vision if not the simple truth that we all need each other's help, and that those of us less in need of help stand to gain a great deal of personal satisfaction if we adopt an attitude of real sympathy towards those more in need.

Notice that I said "adopt an attitude". To some, that phrasing may seem weak, even evasive. But it is not. If the ship is to change its course, to avoid the shoals and reefs *and* to identify a new direction, that can only be accomplished by fundamental changes in attitude. The first and most important of the new attitudes that must be adopted is that *everyone* has a right to life, liberty and the pursuit of happiness, everyone has a right to a political order "of, for and by the people", and those of us who have had the good fortune to be born into a setting which secures many or most of those rights *will only naturally feel satisfaction at helping to extend those rights to everyone.* But, while it will take work to achieve the extension of those rights to everyone, hard work is not the *sine qua non*: commitment to the goal is. Real commitment precedes effective action, and the attitude change progressives must bring about is, at bottom, a commitment, a constant awareness of the injustices that exist in the world and a feeling of dissatisfaction with that state of affairs.

But while the responsibility of the "haves" to the "have-nots" comes naturally to mind for some of us, it would be naïve to think that that sentiment alone would allow the sea-change of attitudes that is called for. Charity is a fragile sentiment, and one that, as we've said already, has an uneasy place in the pantheon of democratic values. What a progressive view must emphasize is the way in which a more affluent, more democratic world will provide the already affluent with a larger, more all-embracing community—and not a little gratitude and appreciation from those who are brought into that community. What is required is no less than a redefinition of the phrase "pursuit of happiness"; the new rallying cry must be "pursuit of satisfaction"—and it is up to progressives to assure that the word "satisfaction" carries with it strong overtones of mutuality and community.

In some respects, this is the most radical, even revolutionary message the progressive mind has to communicate, and it will be seen by many conservatives as the most dangerous. From the corporate world to the small business, howls of protest and derision are likely to be heard if progressives suggest that material gain must take a back seat to concerns of personal satisfaction, and not just in the United States. Tragically, but perhaps inevitably, the explosion of wealth that has taken place in industrial democracies, largely thanks to the industrial and technological revolutions of the last two centuries, has so interwoven itself into our daily lives that, as we have seen, the deeper questions of personal satisfaction have been shunted to one side. Conservatives will say, echoing Fitzgerald's Jay Gatsby, that the matter of personal satisfaction is "strictly personal", that it's not for others to tell us to seek, or where to seek, those satisfactions. But in fact, the explosion of consumer culture that transformed the industrial democracies in the second half of the twentieth century—the transformational spread of everything from appliances to electronic webs across our landscape—*and the complete lack of any notion of when enough is enough* has made increasing acquisition of material wealth the default setting, indeed the required social norm, for members of those industrial societies. So pervasive is the assumption that we will all continue to consume at greater and accelerating levels that anyone who chooses not to do so is seen as an eccentric. And, as we have known for decades, anyone not able to enter the current and roar down the river of wealth with the great mass of their fellows leaves themself open to being judged "a failure" in one form or another.

In other words, we have imposed on ourselves the norm of accelerating material consumption: to claim that a shift to emphasis on personal satisfaction is somehow an intrusion on areas that must be considered personal and private is a fraud. Tired, hollow conservative prohibitions against "interference"— usually governmental—in personal life are most often nothing more than a ruse that disguises a dedication to the "right" of others to profit from our obsession with material acquisition. And those prohibitions become exposed as all the more hollow when one hears conservative cant about things like "family values". Nothing has done more to undermine the ability of a family to cohere in the way conservatives claim they would like to see than the stresses created by the need to maintain a normative level of consumption in modern industrial democracies.

The shift that progressives must call for is the one Erich Fromm spoke of when he distinguished between two kinds of freedom: "freedom from" and "freedom for". [17] The American Dream was built on the belief in the first kind of freedom: freedom from oppression, from want, from insecurity. This has, in fact, been the implied goal of much of the history of humankind, which is why the American Dream—a material and psychological promised land which seemed so close at hand—had such power over those who embraced it. But the American Dream had little to say about what to do with freedom once freedom from want was achieved. Not only did it fail to move people in directions of creative expression which Maslow says can be the consequence of satisfaction of basic needs, it left an entire social order facing the existential crisis of meaning Frankl spoke of, a sense of waiting for something that never arrived. A Democratic Vision would go far to resolve that crisis of meaning, to fill the void created by a life in which a preoccupation with material wealth is practically the only social norm to which the entire social order subscribes.

A Note on National Differences

Needless to say, much of what has been said about the obsession with material wealth and the consequent crisis of meaning is more appropriate to contemporary American society

17 *Escape From Freedom* (New York: Holt, Rinehart and Winston, 1941).

than perhaps any other. European society, in particular, often congratulates itself on the degree to which it eschews the more vulgar forms of conspicuous consumption Americans are, both rightly and wrongly, known for. Europeans pride themselves, for instance, on their appreciation of the arts and the support and respect they extend to them, and that pride is justified. Europeans also pride themselves on the daily forms which they say distinguish them from the mindless workaholism of the American style of life. The French, for instance, point condescendingly to such things as the way Americans will eat a quick sandwich at lunch while they themselves spend two hours enjoying their food, talking with their colleagues and generally soaking up the atmosphere of community on which they thrive; on any given night, ratings agencies show that the majority of the French population is not watching telelvison—largely because they are at the theater, the concert hall, or with friends, probably enjoying another long meal of the kind they had at midday.

But consumer creep has taken place in all the EU countries. Because it has taken place gradually, over a period of half a century, it can be harder to see. However the transformation of the former Soviet bloc countries like Poland, Hungary, Slovakia and the Czech Republic since the revolutions of 1989–90 presents a glaring, almost frightening display of just how universal, and how toxic to such things as personal satisfaction and "family values", the onset of Western affluence and consumer culture has been. Not only has the arrival of everything from McDonald's to SUVs, along with urban sprawl, blighted the landscape; the social traditions which were apparent only a decade and a half ago (many of which had, as I've said, been maintained privately, in homes, under communism, partly as a quiet way of resisting the prohibitions of the regime) have grown thin and threadbare, when they have survived at all.

One of the most poignant illustrations of this thinning of the old social fabric appeared in a 2004 Czech documentary, *Český Sen* ("Czech Dream"), which satirized the wholehearted lunge towards consumer culture that was taking place in the country. In one scene, a family is being interviewed about their weekend activities together, and the mother comments that she insists on the family taking a walk in the nearby forest on weekends— an age-old tradition that takes place in one form or another in countries all over Europe. The 12 year-old daughter hates their hikes, she says, but to "calm her down" the family then goes to the local shopping mall—one hardly distinguishable, except perhaps for its somewhat more modest scale, from many American malls. When the filmmakers query the daughter about why the visit to the mall calms her down, she says "It's as though it was raining—and then I saw the sun come out!"

For decades, the onset of consumerization was attacked as Americanization—"Coca-colismo" in the memorable epithet of the 60s. But it is clear that consumer culture would have emerged with or without America. Once societies of affluence appear, if there is no deeper direction towards which the members of society are striving, then acquisition, and the appearance of progress by virtue of technical innovation, will serve as compass and gyroscope. While in older cultures centuries-old traditions may provide a buffer to these changes, at least for a time, inevitably those traditions are themselves likely to be dissolved by the wave of the new. This fact, and the virulent resistance to it, has not been sufficiently recognized as a force in emergent fundamentalisms all over the world.

VII

We live at a unique intersection in human history. On the one hand, the technological progress which began with language and tool-making thousands of years ago has begun to accelerate exponentially, and with that acceleration has come the expansion of the possibilities of affluence hardly even dreamed of before the twentieth century. At the same time, we are witnessing—almost as a consequence of material success, some would say—an equally precipitious decline in the sense of meaning which has fueled our lives since hominids first began to see patterns of purpose in the world around them.

But this very characterization must itself be subjected to certain qualifications, qualifications which greatly complicate the task of those who would try to come to grips with exactly what this intersection "means". To begin with, the wealth that we see as having exploded across the landscape of human existence in the last century has, in fact, spread its effects in a very limited area: affluence of the kind we associate with Western democracies is accessible to a very small proportion of the planet's population—little more than was the case in pre-democratic societies, when an aristocratic few enjoyed material wealth while the bulk of the population lived in circumstances little changed for centuries, even millenia.

What is measurably different about our age is the fact that many of the ancillary consequences of affluence and technology have had impact on almost everyone on the planet, rich and poor. Everyone has access of some kind to radio, television or the internet, and that access is changing the nature of their perceptions. A new global set of social practices and forms, many of them built around the consumption which is largely available only to the affluent, has emerged and, for many, replaced more traditional forms of culture and belief. This transformation has helped to fuel the fundamentalist reaction to materialism and modernity that was mentioned above.

In other words, affluence and change—or sometimes nothing more than the prospect of the life they hold out for the many who have little of the former but experience a surplus of the latter—have combined to wear away, sometimes furiously, at the fabric of social, religious and family life that have dominated human existence since time immemorial. And they have done so without making even the most fundamental benefits of affluence—adequate food, shelter, clothing, education and security—available to more than a small percentage of the world's population. What's more, the fact that affluence and change have come about without an attendant understanding of how well the biosphere we occupy can support them means that we can't even be certain that an environmental catastrophe of proportions equal to the nuclear holocaust we seem to have evaded in the last century doesn't await us in the foreseeable future.

We live in a time of true crisis. But we are not without resources, the most important of which may be our ability to put our world in perspective.

Two centuries ago—an afternoon stroll in the history of humankind—Western philosophy built its palaces on such scaffolds as as the primacy of power in human affairs, the influence of God's will via the benevolent force of History and the inevitability of dialectic in bringing us to a new millenium. Today, we are vastly less prosaic, and at least somewhat more realistic, in our view of where we are, where we have been, and where to go from here. But we are also in a much more powerful position to see ourselves and our world as we really are. Without launching out into some New Age, Starship Enterprise view of where we must go, we can look at ourselves as a species situated on a habitable planet with sufficient resources, talents and tools to maintain ourselves at a minimum level of comfort and within the limits of those resources.

We have also begun to recognize that our species has an identifiable pattern of needs, behavioral responses to those needs, and even an ability, in the right circumstances, to transcend those needs, and that the insights we have into how our species behaves, brought together with our understanding of our evolution and of the environment we inhabit, afford us the chance to establish an equilibrium which will afford us all safety, security, and the opportunity to reflect on questions of meaning without facing undue threat. What is perhaps most awe-inspring about our age—and, indeed, frightening—is that *we have the power to situate ourselves in the evolution of our species and our planet and to make our decisions accordingly.*

If there is a foundation-level failing in progressive thinking as we enter fully into the twenty-first century, it is in our failure to assemble this picture clearly and unshrinkingly, to communicate it clearly to the electorates that we purport to serve, and to use it as the basis for dialogue, discussion and decision-making.

The baseline assumptions that emerge from such a stock-taking are clear:

Industrial democracies have achieved a level of affluence that is more than sufficient to satisfy anyone's notions of "prosperity" and, in fact, it poses a serious obstacle to our "pursuit of happiness" because of the mindless preoccupation with material wealth that has filled the vacuum in our lives.

The disparity between the wealth of the affluent and the destitution of the poor—a disparity built in part, however unintentionally, on the dependence of the wealthy on the avialability of cheap resources, among them labor, afforded by the poor—is a running sore on the body of the human community which also threatens to reawaken and reinflame massive nation or culture-based conflicts we had hoped had been put to rest in the world wars of the last century.

The ability to understand and absorb this view of our place in human history is well within the ken of many, if not most, in the Western democracies: given the chance, they will be able to listen to and to engage in dialogue and discussion about what the consequences of this view are for policy-setting.

Whatever specific policy actions may be decided upon as a result of true dialogue, both among progressives themselves and with conservatives, they must recognize that security and stability—though not necessarily unbridled affluence—are the only guarantees that humane and democratic attitudes will take root and grow around the world.

The crisis of meaning in the West (and in other cultures, where materialistic goals have overshadowed traditional values) can be filled to no small degree with a gradual but determined shift in our attention from the pursuit of material wealth to the spread of material security. Feelings of community and communality must be generated on both sides of the affluent divide if this is to be accomplished, but, again, given the right leadership, people in democratic societies are capable of making this shift.

These are the principles upon which progressive thinking in the twenty-first century—and beyond—must be based. They are not principles discovered on ancient stone tablets, uncovered in the code of some ancient text, or teased out of erudite theories about patterns in history. They are, in fact, common sense principles based on very palpable and common sense truths about humankind, its evolution and the pivotal moment at which it stands in its history. The only thing for us to do is embrace them and begin a dialogue about what the lessons they represent tell us what we should do next.

Epilogue

One late autumn afternoon, sometime in the mid-Fifties of the last century, as the sun sank through hazy skies towards the horizon and dusk set in, I had what might today be called a "Francis Fukuyama moment".

I had been working on my bicycle and, caught up in the beauty of the afternoon, I began to reflect on the times into which I had been born. Images of my parents' lives—the struggles of the Depression and World War II—must have flashed briefly through my mind, for I saw myself as living in an age when all problems had been solved, all life-and-death struggles had been put behind us, and humankind had finally begun to enjoy the rewards it had worked so long to attain. The world had entered into its own, and I had been fortunate enough to have been born into the epicenter of a new—and, as I saw it, permanent—era of triumphal American tranquility. I was nine years old.

Unfortunately, the satisfaction that came with my reflections on what Fukuyama would call, several decades later, "the end of history", was short-lived.[18] For as I compared my time

18   *The End of History and the Last Man* (New York: Free Press, 1992).

and my country to other triumphal moments in history—the Roman empire came to mind—I realized that people living in other times must also have believed that their moment was supreme and would be unending. And they, even the seemingly all-powerful, invincible Romans, had been wrong: desperately, terribly wrong. So as the dusk deepened into near-twilight, so too did my reflections. Could it be, I asked myself, that all great civilizations inevitably came to an end? Could the same fate befall my own country and my own time? And if so, would all the advances, all the progress, that accompanied my time evaporate too? Could I have been born into an apogee-moment, rather than the transformative new beginning I had imagined only minutes earlier?

An inner chill took hold of me as my thoughts carried me—admittedly in a rather "Little Golden Book" form—through some of the terrain Gibbon and Spengler had covered long before. But unlike them I was saved from any definitive conclusion by my mother's voice calling me to wash for dinner. However the thoughts stayed with me down through the years—over half a century, in fact—as a kind of guiding tension in my view of history, human progress, and America's place in each of those.

Over time, as I became more aware of contemporary history, the Cold War especially, my notion that all life-and-death struggles had been put behind us went by the wayside. Diving from my bicycle in imitation of the "What to Do When the Bomb Strikes" films we were shown in school was a game; living through the Cuban Missile Crisis on a Strategic Air Command base in Central Florida as a teenager was not. And as the Sixties wore on and I saw issues of social justice—racism, poverty, militarism—come to the fore, I knew that all problems had not been solved. In fact, as I matured, I began to see that far more problems remained to be solved than solutions had been found in the "modern" era into which I had been born. And the gifted locale in which I found myself, the US, seemed an island of relative good fortune in a world of struggle and suffering.

But the reflections I'd had on that autumn afternoon years before, and the questions those reflections had led me to, didn't dissipate with the realization that the world was what it was. On the contrary, they lived on as I struggled to come to terms with the questions I'd confronted. There were basically two nodes to that tension. The first lay in the obvious question: Was the ascendancy of the US, perhaps of Western democracy as a whole, nothing but a pinnacle of development that would go into decline—indeed, might already be showing symptoms of decay— as so many other eras in the past had? The other node lay in the question of whether the ascendancy of Western democracy, aided by the phenomenal advancements in relieving human struggle made possible by the technological developments that had accompanied it, could provide the basis for a true transformational moment in which the "boom and bust" cycle of eras and empires could finally be escaped and progress towards a more humane and more enduring world begun.

There are volumes that could be written on these two questions. But pivotal to the question of giving progressive thought a clear sense of direction and purpose is recognizing that our future lies somewhere between them.

There are days, whole months, sometimes, when the spectacle of American life in all its sideshow carnival gaudiness makes me believe that, indeed, it is in decline. Whether measured by the shabbiness of many popular tastes—everything from scandal addiction to tawdry television humor—or more serious symptoms, like the prevalence of drug use, obesity and depression, it is easy to see the US as a society in the stages of early but terminal decadence, thrashing about in the web of material meaninglessness in which it has woven and entangled itself. But there are also times when the notion of transformation seems plausible—not the transformation of some New Age moment in which enlightened thinking erupts across the land like flowers in the spring, but the slow, determined transformation born of deep reflection, honest dialogue and the hard work of taking resolute steps towards goals which gradually coalesce into a world we can confidently call an advance over what has gone before.

Which of these scenarios we choose determines how we act politically. If the former, civilization-in-decline view seems inescapable, then the most we can do is to resign ourselves to the inevitable descent into twilight and fight to limit the amount of suffering produced by the decline, much as Rieux does in Camus' *The Plague*, placing our hopes in the turning of the wheel and the likelihood that it will carry, if not us, then those who come after us back into the light. If we believe in the possibility of transformation, then we struggle to find the path or paths that will take us to, say, the "newer world" Robert Kennedy said we must seek.

The problem is that none among us can say with any certainty that either of these scenarios is more likely than the other; we'd be fools to even try. Nor can we satisfy ourselves with the vague likelihood that the future is likely to fall somewhere in between; true though that may be, it provides us with far too few landmarks to use as we try to navigate our way into so indeterminate a future. One answer would be to find, like Henry Adams, satisfaction in the process, not the goal; but that is a private answer, not one likely to bind people together into groups dedicated to change. An alternative would be to insist that transformation *can* be brought about—that we *must* believe and thereby *make it so*. Clearly the 2008 election was powered in part by this sentiment—and, at least on that occasion, it worked, as seems to have been the case so many times in American history. But this is a distinctly American style of response, looked at askance and even parodied by others, especially Europeans, whose efforts must be united with our own if progressive thinking is to have the global impact it must.

I don't know what Tony Judt felt about these matters: our abbreviated dialogue never allowed us to explore them. But I have a hunch. For while I held onto hopes that Stephen Hawking's survival of ALS might provide a precedent for Tony's, I suspect that Tony did not. (The Irish tradition is full of mystic, sometimes mindless, hope; the Jewish tends to rely on resigned, if sometimes harsh, *amor fati*.) He was dying; he knew it. But why then, one is forced to ask, did he dedicate a considerable part of his last months to a work, *Ill Fares the Land*, which he would likely barely live to see reviewed, let alone see having some wider social or political impact?

There are many possible answers to that question, and no doubt the truth lies in some combination of all of them. Any prominent intellectual values being heard; to have one last conversation with the public, and know it's the last, is an opportunity not to be missed. Tony's mind was clear and energetic to the very end; for him to give up expressing his ideas would have been as unnatural as giving up seeing while he still had sight. And there is, of course, the passionate dedication to social justice and to morality that infused all of his work, a passion that he could not fail to engage until he could do so no more.

But Tony was also a father. He had, as I do, two teenage sons. And, while we never had the opportunity to discuss them, I have no doubt that he thought about their future—especially in his last days, perhaps, as I'm sure my father's father did while tuberculosis wasted away his life many years before ALS took Tony's.

So I suspect that, just as I have countless times in the past, in moments of doubt about the usefulness of writing a book about the inequalities of affluent societies which he would shortly leave, never to revisit, he drew strength from thinking about his sons. While he might not live to see the impact his book would make, while the book might not even have any impact at all, thinking about his sons, their future, and the world that future would play out in must have reminded him of one of the cardinal rules any good parent learns from the moment they know a child is on its way: you don't take chances with your children's welfare.

And in that rule I think there is a lesson for progressive thinkers, particularly those of us who may wonder about the futility of it all. You don't take chances with humanity's future.

More than perhaps any other time in human history we hold the future in our hands. Those of us who lived through the darker moments of the Cold War and the threat of "nuclear winter" that hung over them learned that lesson in varying degrees. Those of us who worry about the degradation of the environment, the role of debt in a world still rampant with abject poverty or the ghastly spectacle of human suffering apparent in every newscast, every newspaper, on every website, have brought that lesson to bear on the contemporary world. But each of those problems, along with the countless others we face, can paralyze us, either in fear, frustration or a sense of futility. Where do you begin? is a question any serious thinker on the Left or the Right can confront, sometimes on a daily basis, when he or she looks at the world we live in.

You begin, as was said at the outset of this discussion, with premises—premises about the value of human life, premises about the progress of human development, premises about what constitutes real quality of life. You move to a recognition that quality of life is built on stability and security, but that neither of those guarantee that those who enjoy them will take the next step: dedicating themselves to deeper, more enduring, even spiritual satisfactions that transcend material well-being. And finally you come to the *ne plus ultra* of progressive thought: that we are all, indeed, one large family, and what we do for ourselves we do for one another, what one of our family lacks we all lack, and that the state of our family is no better than its most needy member. To ignore those truths is to cheat, not only our family, but ourselves; to subscribe to them is to guarantee satisfaction—not happiness, but true satisfaction—in a world with all too few real satisfactions.

And for those of us who sometimes have doubts—and who doesn't?—about the efficacy of our own meager efforts, about the possibility that Western democracies are in decline, a humane world is receding even as we approach it, there is that fall-back caveat known to all loving, caring parents: you don't take chances with your children's welfare. All the world is, indeed, our family; all children are our children; and the future we give to them we give to all children to come. Perhaps our efforts today will make that future transformational; perhaps not. But like any parent, all we can do is to devote ourselves calmly but determinedly to giving all those children the best future we can. If we do, not only will we earn their respect, we will earn our own. And we will establish a precedent for all humankind to come.